ANSELM'S ARGUMENT

The logic of divine existence

ANSELM'S ARGUMENT
The logic of divine existence

Robert Brecher

Gower

© Robert Brecher, 1985
All rights reserved. No part of this publication may be reproduced, stored in a retrieval system, or transmitted in any form or by any means, electronic, mechanical, photocopying, recording or otherwise without the prior permission of Gower Publishing Company Limited.

Published by

Gower Publishing Company Limited,
Gower House,
Croft Road,
Aldershot,
Hants GU11 3HR,
England.

Gower Publishing Company,
Old Post Road,
Brookfield,
Vermont 05036,
U.S.A.

British Library cataloguing in publication data:

Brecher, Robert
   Anselm's argument.
   1. Anselm, *Saint*   2. God – Proof, Ontological
  – History of doctrines – Middle Ages, 600–1500
  I. Title
212'.1'0924   BT100.A5663

ISBN 0 566 050226 X

Printed in Great Britain by
Blackmore Press, Shaftesbury, Dorset

Contents

	Preface	vii
	Introduction	1
1	Anselm's Concept of Greatness	6
2	Necessity and Anselm's Argument	19
3	*Proslogion* II	36
4	'Existence' and God	70
5	God and Necessary Existence	85
6	Conclusion	114
	Notes	117
	Bibliography	128
	Index of names	137

Preface

This book has its origins in a doctoral thesis presented to the University of Kent at Canterbury in 1977, and I should like to thank the many students and teachers who offered encouragement and criticism while I was working on it. In particular I am indebted to Professor Alec Whitehouse, without whose inspiration I might never have started at all; and to Christopher Cherry, with whom I spent many hours in constructively critical discussion. For his time-consuming guidance, painstaking analysis, and unfailing encouragement, both as my supervisor and since, I am deeply grateful; and also for his valuable comments on the final draft. Needless to say, of course, the errors and deficiencies remain my own.

Much of the research was made possible by grants from the Department of Education & Science, the Worshipful Company of Leathersellers, and the Sir Richard Stapley Educational Trust; publication costs were met by a grant from the British Academy. To all these bodies I extend my thanks.

Part of ch. 1 has appeared in *Philosophical Quarterly*, 24 (1974), pp. 97–105, as '"Greatness" in Anselm's Ontological Argument', and part of ch. 3 in *Philosophical Studies* (Eire), XXIII (1975), pp. 63–66, as 'Aquinas on Anselm'. I am grateful to the editors of these journals for permission to make use of this material: also to the respective publishers for permission to make use of *St. Anselm's 'Proslogion' with 'A Reply on Behalf of the Fool' and 'The Author's Reply to Gaunilo'*, translated with an introduction and philosophical commentary by M. J. Charlesworth (Oxford University Press, 1965), for translations of Anselm's *Proslogion* and *Reply*, and Gaunilo's *Reply*; and *St. Anselm: Basic Writings*, translated by S. N. Deane (Open Court, La Salle, Ill. 1962, 2nd. ed.), for translations of the *Monologion* and *Cur Deus Homo*. All references in the text are to these editions. The only alteration I have made is to omit the hyphens Charlesworth inserts into Anselm's formula.

Finally I should like to thank Keren Patterson for her extremely efficient typing of the manuscript.

Robert Brecher
January 1984
Brighton Polytechnic

Introduction

That God truly exists

Well then, Lord, You who give understanding to faith, grant me that I may understand, as much as You see fit, that You exist as we believe You to exist, and that You are what we believe You to be. Now we believe that You are something than which nothing greater can be thought. Or can it be that a thing of such a nature does not exist, since 'the Fool has said in his heart, there is no God' [Ps. xiii. I, lii. I]? But surely, when this same Fool hears what I am speaking about, namely, 'something than which nothing greater can be thought', he understands what he hears, and what he understands is in his mind, even if he does not understand that it actually exists. For it is one thing for an object to exist in the mind, and another thing to understand that an object actually exists. Thus, when a painter plans beforehand what he is going to execute, he has [the picture] in his mind, but he does not yet think that it actually exists because he has not yet executed it. However, when he has actually painted it, then he both has it in his mind and understands that it exists because he has now made it. Even the Fool, then, is forced to agree that something than which nothing greater can be thought exists in the mind, since he understands this when he hears it, and whatever is understood is in the mind. And surely that than which a greater cannot be thought cannot exist in the mind alone. For if it exists solely in the mind even, it can be thought to exist in reality also, which is greater. If then that than which a greater cannot be thought exists in the mind alone, this same that than which a greater *cannot* be thought is that than which a greater *can* be thought. But this is obviously impossible. Therefore there is absolutely no doubt that something than which a greater cannot be thought exists both in the mind and in reality.

—*Proslogion* II

That God cannot be thought not to exist

And certainly this being so truly exists that it cannot be even thought not to exist. For something can be thought to exist that cannot be thought not to exist, and this is greater than that which can be thought not to exist. Hence, if that than which a greater cannot be thought can be thought not to exist, then that than which a greater cannot be thought is not the same as that than which a greater cannot be thought, which is absurd. Something than which a greater cannot be thought exists so truly then, that it cannot be even thought not to exist.

And You, Lord our God, are this being. You exist so truly, Lord my God, that You cannot even be thought not to exist. And this is as it should be, for if some intelligence could think of something better than You, the creature would be above its creator and would judge its creator — and that is completely absurd. In fact, everything else there is, except You alone, can be thought of as not existing. You alone, then, of all things most truly exist and therefore of all things possess existence to the highest degree; for anything else does not exist as truly, and so possesses existence to a lesser degree. Why then did 'the Fool say in his heart, there is no God' [Ps. xiii. I, lii. I] when it is so evident to any rational mind that You of all things exist to the highest degree? Why indeed, unless because he was stupid and a fool?

—Prosolgion III

How 'the Fool said in his heart' what cannot be thought

How indeed has he 'said in his heart' what he could not think; or how could he not think what he 'said in his heart', since to 'say in one's heart' and to 'think' are the same? But if he really (indeed, since he really) both thought because he 'said in his heart' and did not 'say in his heart' because he could not think, there is not only one sense in which something is 'said in one's heart' or thought. For in one sense a thing is thought when the word signifying it is thought; in another sense when the very object which the thing is is understood. In the first sense, then, God can be thought not to exist, but not at all in the second sense. No one, indeed, understanding what God is can think that God does not exist, even though he may say these words in his heart either without any [objective] signification or with some peculiar signification. For God is that than which nothing greater can be thought. Whoever really understands this understands clearly that this same being so exists that not even in thought can it not exist. Thus whoever understands that God exists in such a way cannot think of Him as not existing.

I give thanks, good Lord, I give thanks to You, since what I believed before through Your free gift I now so understand

through Your illumination, that if I did not want to *believe* that You existed, I should nevertheless be unable not to *understand* it.
—*Proslogion* IV

St. Anselm — monk, Church politician, Archbishop of Canterbury, theologian-philosopher of penetrating subtlety — wrote these few lines in 1078, as part of a short treatise, the *Proslogion*, which his fellow-monks had asked him to produce as an example of meditation about the rational basis of faith. Ch. II in particular has since given rise to a greater volume of philosophical effort than perhaps any other single argument. Anselm's argument elicited an immediate response from Gaunilo, a monk from Marmoutier, to which Anselm replied directly. Gaunilo's *Reply on Behalf of the Fool* and Anselm's *Reply to Gaunilo* were circulated together with the *Proslogion* at Anselm's suggestion. Thereafter the argument lay dormant throughout the twelfth century, to be revived, whether in Anselm's own or in some corrupt version, by Richard Fishacre and Alexander of Hales. Among the later scholastics, Aquinas rejected it, while Bonaventure and Duns Scotus incorporated it into their philosophical theology. Descartes produced a similar, though grossly inferior, argument, which was taken up by Spinoza and developed by Leibniz (who expressed a central insight in arguing that 'If God is possible, God exists') and repudiated by Hobbes, Gassendi, *et al.* Kant's apparent demolition of Descartes' version was until recently thought by many to have finally disposed of any *a priori* argument for the existence of God. An Anselmian formulation, however, occupied a key role in Hegel's thought, and the argument enjoyed a brief renaissance among the British idealists, especially Edward Caird. Thereafter it was overwhelmed by logical positivism in the Anglo-Saxon world, although attracting increasing attention on the continent by writers such as Gilson, Barth, and Koyré. The recent revival sparked off largely by Charles Hartshorne has led to such a spate of books and articles in the last fifteen years that a complete bibliography would occupy half a volume itself.[1]

Why, then, add to this mass of material? Despite their valuable contribution in certain areas of debate, Hartshorne and Malcolm have foisted onto Anselm an argument not his own in "relocating" it in ch. III and regarding ch. II as a poor first attempt. Others have offered interpretations varying from the highly persuasive but finally unconvincing Anselm, unconvincing because presented with too much Wittgensteinian hindsight, of Richard Campbell[2] to the extraordinary contortions of Richard R. La Croix, who insists that Anselm is not really trying to prove the existence of *God* at all, and that it is the entire *Proslogion* which constitutes Anselm's effort not to do so.[3] Barth and others have proposed a 'purely theological' interpretation, arguing that there is strictly speaking no philosophical argument at all in the *Proslogion*, but only an exposition of belief.[4] And there are many who insist that the argument should have been given a burial, decent or otherwise, long ago.

I think, however, that there is an interpretation of Anselm's argument which at once does justice to his thought; shows the argument to be valid but not probative; explains why it has refused to lie down despite the apparent finality of many dismissals; and displays in so doing both the structural basis of the Christian doctrine of God and its own importance for understanding that doctrine. It is a magnifying glass through which may be clearly seen the nature of the central problems about the Christian assertion that there is a God. Doubtless these are very large claims. Doubtless they will be challenged, and rightly so. Nevertheless, nothing less than a conviction that they are at least broadly right would justify the enterprise.

Anselm's argument, I maintain, is to be understood in the context of its author's platonic metaphysics. The interpretation is generous to Anselm in that it justifies much that may otherwise appear problematic in the *Proslogion* and *Reply*, but it is consistent both with his broader philosophical orientation and the tradition whose 'God' the argument concerns. If attention is paid to arriving at a proper understanding of what Anselm actually means when he writes that God is 'that than which nothing greater can be thought', and that it is 'greater' to exist 'in reality also' than 'solely in the mind', it becomes clear that his thought is thoroughly platonic.[5] This in turn permits a proper assessment of the validity or otherwise of the argument, whereupon it becomes clear that the argument of ch. II is valid, given the premises, but that it fails to prove that God indeed exists because these premises are problematic. It is Anselm's natural assumption of a relatively unproblematic identity between the God of Christianity and the *ens realissimum* of platonism which has, in part, brought about the failure of commentators — from Gaunilo to Kant — to give proper consideration to the nature of the existence at stake. And it is this failure which lies at the heart of the perennial fascination exercised by the argument. For supporters of the argument have been right to be impatient of the often shallow and dogmatic objections put forward by its opponents: surely the reality of the *ens realissimum* is undeniable. On the other hand, objectors are right to reject an argument which, hanging something as momentous as the existence of God upon a few lines of argument, apparently generates an existential conclusion from a mere idea. The seeming irreconcilability of such vastly different responses to the argument arises from the failure to see that Anselm's definition of God is one which identifies him as the supreme reality of a hierarchical ontology, a failure which in turn obscures the logic of his argument. We can be satisfied, therefore, neither with the position that God is God, therefore he exists,[6] nor with the view that 'Were not the thought so cursedly acute/One might be tempted to declare it silly'.[7] The argument's conflation of religious doctrine with Greek metaphysics reflects just such a conflation within Christianity itself, one which in turn gives rise to the central difficulty about its concept of God — namely its very intelligibility. In analysing Anselm's premisses, then, their relation to the form of the argument, and their place in the Christian thinking about God, we uncover the fundamental problems involved in asserting God's existence. Indeed, the fact that the argument is formally valid itself tells us a good deal about 'God', and indicates what is centrally problematic about the concept. The ideal of the timeless truth, eternally valid, which Plato is said to have dreamed of, has been appropriated by Christianity. It has thus inherited the problem of showing what possible relation to the world something could have, the existence of which conforms to such an ideal. In leading to the conclusion that the question of the existence of God is one and the same as that of the possibility of speaking coherently about God, a possibility which Anselm did not basically question, his argument is a faithful and centrally illustrative reflection of Christian doctrine.

Chapter 1

Anselm's concept of greatness

Anselm's argument in *Proslogion* II begins with the words, 'Now we believe that You are something than which nothing greater [maius] can be thought'. It is usually assumed by commentators that 'maius' is interchangeable with 'melius', and that for 'greater' we can read 'better', or, even more oddly, 'more perfect'. This quite unjustified assumption has prevented even those who are in other respects most meticulous in their exegesis of Anselm's text from coming to a proper appreciation of his argument's metaphysical context. Both its structure and purpose become obscured if 'maius' and 'melius' are conflated.[1]

The word 'maius' occurs nine times in ch. II of the *Proslogion*, and 'melius' not at all; in ch. III 'maius' occurs five times, 'melius' once; in ch. IV 'maius' occurs once, 'melius' not at all. The argument having been concluded, Anselm discusses, in the remaining chapters, what God is like. In ch. V he asks, 'What then are You, Lord God, You than whom nothing greater can be thought?', and answers '...that supreme being, existing through Yourself alone, who made everything else from nothing' (p. 121). From this, he begins to draw out God's nature:

> What goodness, then, could be wanting to the supreme good, through which every good exists? Thus You are just, truthful, happy and whatever it is better ['melius'] to be than not to be — for it is better ['melius'] to be just rather than unjust, and happy rather than unhappy. —ibid.

This chapter is important because it shows that, far from using 'maius' and 'melius' interchangeably, Anselm was generally careful to distinguish between them. And it is 'maius' which he uses in *Proslogion* II—IV, with a single exception which I shall discuss presently. God's being 'melius' follows from his being the supreme 'bonum'. His being the supreme good follows from the fact that every good exists through him, since he made everything else from nothing. And it is because he is the creator, the ground of all being, that he is 'that than whom nothing greater can be thought'. This distinction between God's ontological supremacy and his goodness is retained throughout the *Proslogion*.

In ch. IX Anselm discusses God's moral goodness, his 'bonitas'; and no mention is made of his greatness. In ch. XIII we read:

> All that which is enclosed in any way by place or time is less ['minus'] than that which no law of place or time constrains. Since, then, nothing is greater ['maius'] than You, no place or time confines You, but You exist everywhere and always. —p. 133.

The ontological qualities of being independent of time and place constitute greatness — not goodness. In ch. XV, when Anselm returns to the subject of God's greatness, and, incidentally, to the more philosophical tone of chs. II—IV, as distinct from the more religious, or adorational tone of the rest of the *Proslogion*, he again describes God as 'maius', not 'melius'. In ch. XVIII, Anselm says he is life, wisdom, truth, goodness, blessedness, eternity, and every true good — but not that he is greatness. God's greatness is in a different class from his virtues, and this is seen again in ch. XXII. Ch. XXIII concludes:

> 'Moreover, one thing is necessary' [Luke, X, 42]. This is, *moreover*, that one thing necessary in which is every good, or rather, which is wholly and uniquely and completely and solely good.
> —p. 147 (my italics)

Once again, goodness is distinguished from an ontological quality.

What, however, of the single occurrence of 'melius' in ch. III? The context in which it occurs is one where Anselm is saying that God 'cannot even be thought not to exist', which 'is as it should be, for if some intelligence could think of something better ["melius"]...the creature would be above its creator — and that is completely absurd' (p. 119). In view of the mass of evidence from the rest of the *Proslogion*, it is reasonable to conclude that Anselm allows the notion of *judging* to mislead him into writing 'melius' here instead of 'maius'. This argument as to why God cannot be thought not to exist gains such force as it has, of course, from the notion of the supposed absurdity of creature *judging* creator, which notion in turn makes clearer sense if applied to the idea of the creature thinking of something morally better, as opposed to something greater, than God, something morally better which the creature could use as a yardstick with which to judge God. Had Anselm been more careful here, this argument would not have been open to him until after ch. V — not that he needs it anyway, since the point that God cannot be thought not to exist receives sufficient attention at the beginning of ch. III. What this does show is that 'greater' and 'better' are indeed closely linked, as Anselm later argues, following the Platonic tradition.

Throughout his replies to Gaunilo's objections to the argument, Anselm talks of something's being better, rather than greater, only once. It could be argued that in the passage where he presses an analogy between the mind's ability to mount 'from the less good to the more good', and our being able to 'conjecture a great deal about that than which a greater cannot be thought' (*Reply* VIII, p. 187), Anselm fails to observe the distinction between greatness and goodness. However, since this is the sole example of such a use of 'melius' in the entire *Reply*, as against an otherwise consistent use of 'maius', and since it is not absolutely clear that the distinction is in fact blurred here, I do not think it seriously damaging to my argument. Moreover, it is a view confirmed by Anselm's reply to Gaunilo's alleged counter-example of the 'Lost Island', as I shall presently argue.

A general principle to the effect that whatever exists is better than anything which does not exist would be exceedingly difficult to substantiate. As Charlesworth points out it is not at all clear that, for example, an actual evil is better than an imagined one;[2] nor, following Malcolm, is it clear that my future house will be better if it exists than if it does not.³ Clearly Hitler was not better than King Arthur. Or, if it is objected that only one who exists can, properly speaking, be good anyway — a temptation to be avoided — and that existents cannot be compared with non-existent beings in terms of goodness, then Hitler could not be either better or worse than King Arthur, since the latter could not have any moral qualities at all. If Anselm had intended to propound the highly dubious thesis that an existing God is better than a non-existent one, then why not write 'melius' rather than 'maius'? What sense would such an interpretation allow to ch. V? And what if, for example, some of the gods of the Hindu pantheon actually existed? Would Anselm be committed to saying that they were *better* than the Christian, or Jewish, or Moslem God, if he *were* a figment of man's imagination?

Turning to consider 'more perfect', the difficulties mutiply. First, there is that of taking existence itself to be a perfection, as did Descartes. Apart from the perhaps problematic implication of this that existence is a property, it is anyway by no means clear that existence need be chief among perfections, or that it need be a perfection at all. Why could it not in some instances be outweighed by perfections possessed by non-existent entities? To say that existence is a perfection is not to say that it is a perfection in the absence of which no other perfections are possible; and to argue the latter would be plainly ridiculous. A superbly-crafted character in a novel might well be considered perfect, a certain living person imperfect in many respects: a completed building might well be imperfect as compared with its appearance on the architect's drawing board. To avoid these problems, Anselm's thesis, that to exist in reality is greater than to exist in the mind alone, would have to be understood as applying uniquely to God. But even this would not help, for it is no clearer that an existing God must be more perfect than a non-existent one, than that he must be better than a non-existent one. Anyway, the two Gods being compared would have to be alike in all other respects, save that one existed and the other did not (in view of what is said above). This is in fact a thesis that some commentators have attributed to Anselm.⁴ But in what sense is 'more perfect' being used here? If it means simply 'better', that is, 'morally better', then that, as we have seen, solves nothing. If not, then what does it mean?

'More perfect' may perhaps be taken to mean morally better, or more beautiful, or better fitted for a specific purpose, or possibly one or two other things; but it is not, unlike 'yellow' or Moore's 'good', simple and indefinable. If a thing is perfect, then it is perfect in some particular respect or respects. Indeed, Anselm discusses the various respects in which God is perfect in chs. V — XXV of the *Proslogion* — after having established, to his own satisfaction at least, his existence. And of course, it cannot be existence, or manner, or degree, of existence with respect to which God is said to be perfect in the proof of his existence, since that really would be to beg the question. There is, then, no good reason why something 'than which nothing more perfect can be thought' should have to exist in order that that description should fit it, since, once 'more perfect' has been given a definite sense — if indeed it can be given a definite sense — it becomes clear that existence need not be a feature of whatever it is that is said to be 'more perfect'. The phrase could, of course, be given some such sense as 'existing to a higher degree', but in this context such a move is clearly illicit.

Having ruled out 'better' and 'more perfect' as glosses on 'greater', it remains to establish what Anselm actually does mean by 'maius'. In ch. III Anselm says that God *'so truly exists'* that he cannot be thought not to exist. This phrase is repeated three times, and Anselm goes on:

> You alone, then, of all things *most truly exist* and therefore of all things possess existence *to the highest degree*; for anything else does not exist *as truly*, and so possesses existence *to a lower degree*...You of all things exist *to the highest degree*.
>
> —p.119 (my italics)

Allowing Anselm the notion of something's possessing existence, and treating it as an (unfortunate) equivalent of something's existing, as Anselm himself does in the penultimate sentence of the chapter, this passage is surely clear evidence that he was conducting his argument within a context of platonic metaphysics; a framework which, unlike contemporary fashions, admits of the notion of degrees of existence.

Anselm drew much of his theology from Augustine, and

whether his description of God as 'that than which nothing greater can be thought' derives from Augustine or Seneca, both of whom used it, his philosophical and theological framework is that of Augustine, with whose work he was thoroughly familiar, and whom he regarded as his mentor.[5] Augustine himself was, of course, influenced to a great extent by neo-platonism, and especially by Plotinus. In his excellent article '"Vere esse" im *Proslogion* des hl. Anselm',[6] Stolz traces the notion of God's existing so truly that he cannot be thought not to exist through the works of Augustine, and makes it quite clear that Anselm was working with one and the same notion. '*Vere esse*,' Stolz writes, 'thus describes for Augustine the absolute, unchanging, divine being...';[7] and 'over against this divine, unchanging being stands the subdued being of creatures, subject to change, which contains something of not-being in itself, and which is therefore not "vere"... In this conception of St. Augustine's, the influence of neo-platonic philosophy is revealed very clearly',[8] an influence to which Augustine himself admits; in fact, he thinks that Plato must have known the Old Testament.[9] And, as Stolz says, 'Anselm, in his conception of God's being, moves entirely within Augustinian thought: it is unchangeableness which makes God's being absolute being, subsisting reality, so that from the point of view of this determination of being, the thought of God's non-existence is absurd; so that God "most truly exists and possesses existence to the highest degree"'.[10]

Anselm's *Monologion* also makes extensive use of the notion of degrees of existence. In his acute analysis in ch. VIII of the term 'nothing', where he rejects as 'always false' the idea that 'this very nothing...[is]...some existent being' (p. 54), he suggests that 'nothing' and 'something' are not different in kind, but only in degree:

> For, indeed, from the very word that we use, saying that it [the creative Being] *created* them or that they were *created*, we understand that when this Being created them, it created something, and that when they were created, they were created only as something. For so, beholding a man of very lowly fortunes exalted with many riches and honours by someone, we say, 'Lo, he has made that man out of nothing'; that is, the man who was before reputed as nothing is now, by virtue of that other's making, reckoned as something. —p. 55

Non-existent beings '...were not nothing, so far as the creator's thought is concerned, through which, and according to which, they were created' (p. 56) before they came into being. Whatever is 'in the thought', that is, lies along the same continuum as that real object to which it corresponds; the creator changes its state ('the beings that were created...were not what they are now') rather than bringing it into being out of 'absolutely nothing'. Now, whatever the virtues or otherwise of this as a doctrine of *creatio ex nihilo*, or as the apparent positing of some other class besides the class of what exists and the class of what does not exist, it affords further evidence that we may most fruitfully understand Anselm as propounding a theory involving the notion of degrees of existence. Indeed, he actually says that the creator is 'a certain Substance existing in the greatest degree of all existing beings' (p. 53). In his discussion of the relation of the Word to created beings, Anselm says of the Word that its 'essence exists so supremely that in a certain sense it alone exists; while in these things which, in comparison with that Essence, are in some sort non-existent, and yet were made something through, and according to, that Word, a kind of imitation of that supreme Essence is found' (ch. XXXI, p. 92). This surely cannot be anything but platonic language; and the Theory of Forms comes to mind again when Anselm writes:

> If we should conceive any substance that is alive, and sentient, and rational, to be deprived of its reason, then of its sentience, then of its life, and finally of the bare existence that remains, who would fail to understand that the substance that is thus destroyed, little by little, is gradually brought to smaller and smaller degrees of existence, and at last to non-existence? But the attributes which, taken each by itself, reduce an essence to less and less degrees of existence, if assumed in order, lead it to greater and greater degrees.
> —ibid.

Or again:

> But since...all other beings, in accordance with some cause, have at some time been, or will be, by mutation, what they are not now; or what they were not, or will not be, at some time; and, since this former existence of theirs is no longer a fact; and their existence in a transient, and most brief, and scarcely existing, present is hardly a fact — since, then, they exist in such mutability, it is not unreasonably denied that they exist simply, and perfectly, and absolutely; and it is asserted that they are almost non-existent, that they scarcely exist at all.
> —*Monologion* XXVIII, p. 88

It is abundantly clear that Anselm was employing platonic metaphysics in the *Monologion*; and there is no reason to suppose that he repudiated his platonism between finishing the *Monologion* and writing the *Proslogion*.

'Greater' is therefore to be understood in a platonic manner; not as 'better', or 'more perfect', but as 'ontologically greater', that is to say, 'more real'. Once this is established, it becomes possible to do justice to Anselm's argument; and all that has been written about the incomparability in terms of goodness or perfection of real and imaginary things must be dismissed as irrelevant. The question, '...in what sense can we say that actual existents are greater *absolutely* than possible or conceptual existents?'[11] admits of a ready answer: actual existents are more real than possible or conceptual existents. And Malcolm's comment about the oddity of maintaining that my future house will be better if it exists than if it does not (p. 8) fails to touch Anselm.

Now, what is this platonic manner of understanding 'greater'? Plato has a hierarchical view of reality (where 'reality' covers all that there is, those things which are not ontologically independent of human thought, as well as those that are): some things are more real than others. But clearly 'real' cannot refer in this *latter* phrase to all there is. What then does it mean? If we draw on the Divided Line analogy in the *Republic* (509e) we may represent Plato's view of the ontological structure of things thus:

```
↑Forms
|The material world
|Non-existents
```

It is this picture which Anselm uses. And what makes the Forms more real than the material world, which is in turn more real than non-existents, is that, as Vlastos suggests,[12] it is the Forms which are of supreme cognitive reliability, and thus of supreme value. It is cognitive reliability and value which determine degree of reality for Plato. This is in turn the case because cognitive reliability is a sign of ontological independence; and the greater the ontological independence of an entity, the more fully can it be what it is, because the greater is the extent to which it is able to determine itself. For Plato, 'to be completely means to be a complete and perfect essence, to possess in a perfect manner the actuality of essence'.[13] Thus it is aseity which is the mark of what is most real. And that is precisely what Anselm too holds: 'that which exists through itself exists in the greatest degree of all things'.[14] The Forms exist *a se*; the empirical world is finite and dependent on the Forms (or, ultimately, on the Good, which is the supreme Form[15]); and non-existents are those things which are entirely dependent for their being real at all on finite, dependent beings. That is to say, they are fictions, appearing in poetry, people's fancy, etc. They *are* only insofar as they have been thought of or imagined.

The distinction between fictions and non-fictions is crucial for the thesis I am putting forward. When Anselm tries to show the Fool that he is contradicting himself in denying that there is a God, his intention is clearly to show that God cannot be a fiction, for it is just this which the Fool implies when he says 'There is no God'. Now this may seem somewhat obvious. However, in view of the volume of literature about the logic of 'existence' to which the ontological argument has given rise, the point cannot be over-emphasized. What one's view is of the concept of existence matters not at all for an assessment of Anselm's argument — as I shall argue in ch. 4. One needs simply to remember that Anselm seeks to show, as against the unbeliever, that God is not a figment of the imagination, not something invented, in short, not a fiction; and that to do this he uses the platonic principle that non-fictions are more real than fictions. Of course the matter is more complicated than this, and discussion of just what we may understand by 'God is not a fiction', and under what conditions it may intelligibly, let alone truly, be asserted, will form a major portion of what I have to say about Anselm's argument.

Before proceeding further, however, it is as well to allay any suspicion that the platonic ontological scale has a fundamentally axiological basis, so that the distinction I have drawn between 'better' and 'more real' must collapse. The point is that the Good is good because it is ontologically independent: the Forms have supreme value because of their ontological supremacy, and not vice-versa. Whether this traditional inference of value from ontological status is valid is of course another matter, but one which need not concern us here. What is important is that Anselm follows this tradition in arguing *to* God's goodness *from* his supreme reality. This is clearest in ch. XII of the *Proslogion*:

> But clearly, whatever You are, You are not that through another but through Your very self. You are therefore the very life by which You live, the Wisdom by which You are wise, the very goodness by which You are good to both good men and wicked, and the same holds for like attributes. —p. 133

And in ch. III of the *Monologion* we read:

> But whatever exists through another is less than that, through which all things are, and which alone exists through itself. Therefore, that which exists through itself exists in the greatest degree of all things. There is, then, some one being which alone exists in the greatest and the highest degree of all. But that which is greatest of all, and through which exists whatever is good or great, and, in short, whatever has any existence — that must be supremely good, and supremely great, and the highest of all existing beings.[16] —pp. 42–3

It is clear, then, that Anslem regards God's greatness as logically prior to his goodness — which is why 'goodness' plays no significant part in chs. II — IV of the *Proslogion*, being deduced from God's ontological supremacy in ch. V, the first of a long list of attributes so deduced in chs. V — XXV.

Now that is has been established what Anselm means by 'greater', Gaunilo's classic 'Lost Island' "counterexample" can be seen to be as irrelevant as Anselm takes it to be; and all similar objections to Anselm's argument can be dismissed along with it. Gaunilo's argument may be put as follows:[17]

(1) The idea of a Lost Island 'which is more excellent than all other lands' is intelligible.
(2) The Lost Island is therefore in the mind.
(3) 'Since it is more excellent to exist not only in the mind but also in reality', the Lost Island exists in reality;
(4) 'For if it did not exist, any other land existing in reality would be more excellent than it, and so this island, already conceived by you to be more excellent than others, will not be more excellent.'
(5) Anselm's argument, therefore, would prove the existence of anything which is first deemed to be the most excellent of its kind.

The contention that if one starts with any suitably defined fiction, one can think it into existence by following the lines of the ontological argument, has long been a standard objection. Gassendi,[18] Caterus,[19] Schopenhauer,[20] and Reichenbach,[21] among many others, have all taken this line of attack. Yet Anselm hardly bothers to reply to this apparently devastating criticism levelled by Gaunilo, saying simply that '...if anyone should discover for me something existing either in reality or in the mind alone — except "that than which a greater cannot be thought" — to which the logic of my argument would apply, then I shall find that Lost Island and give it, never more to be lost, to that person' (*Reply* III, p. 175). The apparent oddity of this is regarded by many as of no particular importance. Jonathan Barnes,[22] for example, while actually citing a small extract from Bonaventure's amplification of Anselm's reasoning, for which Barnes thinks there is nothing to be said, and which he thinks has nothing to do with Anselm, fails to notice the significance of the reply for an interpretation of the argument. In fact, Bonaventure's amplification is precisely to the point, and worth quoting in full:

> Against the objection of an island than which nothing better or greater can be conceived, we must say that there is no similarity [between this subject and this predicate]. For when I say 'a being than which nothing greater can be conceived', there is no repugnance here between the subject and the predicate, so that this being can be conceived in a rational way. But when I say 'an island than which nothing greater can be conceived', there is a repugnance between the subject and the predicate. For 'island' refers to a defective being, while the predicate designates the most perfect of beings. Therefore, since there is a direct opposition here, this island is conceived irrationally, and in thinking it the mind is divided against itself. It is no wonder, therefore, that we cannot infer that this island exists in reality. It is otherwise, however, in the case of 'being' or 'God', since this is not repugnant to the predicate.[23]

Although failing to distinguish perfection from greatness, and putting the matter somewhat dramatically, Bonaventure clearly has in mind ontological greatness. And the idea of an island which enjoys *ontological* supremacy, which is more cognitively reliable and more valuable, because less existentially dependent, than any other island, is nonsense. No island can 'exist more truly' than another. The Form of Island may perhaps be said to exist more truly than any particular island, but that is another matter. No island, no golden mountain, no coin which is or might be in the world is any less dependent in its existence than any other. Empirical entities and God are in different ontological classes; and whereas 'greater' in the phrase, 'an island, than which *a* greater cannot be thought' serves to compare it with other members of its own class — if it serves to do anything at all — in the phrase, 'a being, than which *nothing* greater can be thought', it serves to compare that being not only with other beings, but, more importantly, the class of which that being is the sole member with all other classes. The phrase, 'an island, than which *nothing* greater can be thought', is absurd, since there could not possibly be any such island: islands are not that sort of thing. In (1) above, therefore, there is no parallel between a Lost Island and God; (3) as it stands is false, and if 'more excellent' were amended to 'greater', then the reasoning in (4) could not apply to islands or the like. (5) is therefore not the case. Anselm, working within a platonic metaphysic, had no need of any further argument against Gaunilo on this point.

Pari rationis, the form of Anselm's argument cannot be used for the sort of "ontological" disproof (or proof) of the devil which has recently been proposed. Neither C. K. Grant's remark that '...if it is supposed that existence is one of the properties comprised in the concept of perfection, then nonexistence must be a property of a completely imperfect being',[24] nor R. J. Richman's opposite view, that if 'I have in my mind the idea of a being than which nothing more evil can be conceived...[then]...if this being exists in reality it is more evil than if it exists only in the mind...[so that]... such a being (called "the Devil") exists (in reality)'[25] have anything at all to do with Anselm's argument. For Anselm is not concerned to argue to God's existence on the basis of his perfection or supreme goodness. His point is that God is the most real entity conceivable; and that non-fictions are more real than fictions. Thus any argument of the same form in respect of the devil's non-existence would have to start as follows: the devil is that than which nothing less real can be thought. But of course, whatever the devil may be, this he clearly is not. Any proof of the devil's existence would have to be based on a comparison of existent with non-existent evil in terms of degree of evil. But this is just the sort of comparison which Malcolm and others rightly reject, and which I have shown is absent from Anselm's argument.

Chapter 2

Necessity and Anselm's argument

The attempt by Hartshorne and Malcolm to relocate Anselm's argument in ch. III of the *Proslogion*, and to present a reinterpretation of Anselm in modal terms, focuses attention on the role of necessity in the argument. Just as an assessment of Anselm's argument requires a proper understanding of his concept of greatness, so it requires a proper understanding of his modal terminology. For not only does the question of whether there is more than one independent argument for the existence of God in the *Proslogion* and *Reply* depend on it, but, as I shall argue in ch. 5, such an understanding helps clarify certain logical features of 'that than which nothing greater can be thought'. I shall consider first the varieties of 'necessity' in Anselm, using *Cur Deus Homo* and the *Monologion* to supplement the *Proslogion* and *Reply*, and then examine what Anselm means when he says that 'God cannot be thought not to exist', so as to make clear his own conception of the relationship between *Proslogion* II and III. If this seems a somewhat tedious exercise, I think it is nevertheless worthwhile, if only because of the considerable influence of the Hartshorne-Malcolm interpretation of Anselm, which although resulting in valuable insights regarding the implications of his argument, is exegetically inaccurate.

In *Cur Deus Homo*, II, XVIII(a), Anselm distinguishes between 'antecedent' and 'subsequent' necessity. Of the former he says:

> ...necessity is always either compulsion or restraint; and these

> two kinds of **necessity** operate variously by turn, so that the same thing is both necessary and impossible. For whatever is obliged to exist is also prevented from non-existence; and that which is compelled not to exist is prevented from existence. —p. 274

This notion of necessity is conceived in terms of coercion or constraint; Anselm contrasts it with 'free authority' (II, XVII, p. 270). In this sense, if a person's action is necessary, or performed of necessity, then the point is that he is unable to act otherwise owing to some external imposition: 'Since, then, the will of God does nothing by any necessity, but of its own power, and the will of that man [Christ] was the same as the will of God, he died not necessarily, but only of his own power' (p. 272). The will of God cannot be coerced or constrained. This may be termed 'factual' rather than 'logical': it is a matter of fact that '...God does nothing by necessity, since he is not compelled or restrained in anything' (II, V, p. 244).[1] Clearly the coercion or constraint in question here is not a matter of logic; Hartshorne and Malcolm cannot, therefore, base any modal reinterpretation of Anselm on his 'antecedent' necessity. Anselm also uses 'necessity' in the context of discussions of purpose, in a way apparently consistent with this usage. For it could plausibly be maintained that the purpose in question in the following sorts of example acts as a coercive force, in some mental sense:

> ...I am rather inclined to the belief that there was not, originally, that complete number of angels necessary to perfect the celestial state... —*Cur Deus Homo*, I, XVIII, p. 214

and

> ...where these [words] are, no other word is necessary for the recognition of an object.[2] —*Monologion*, X, p. 57

The notion of necessity appears in Anselm in a causal sense too:

> And this question, both infidels are accustomed to bring up against us...and many believers ponder it in their hearts; for what cause or necessity, in sooth, God became man... —*Cur Deus Homo*, I, 1, p. 178

In the first two examples, that necessitates x, for which to take place, or for which to be the case, it is necessary that x; and in the latter, the cause of x necessitates it. In this way, then, there is a coercive element in the situation. But whether perspicuous or not, neither of these usages has anything to do with logical necessity.

Subsequent necessity, 'that necessity which Aristotle treats of (*"de propositionibus singularibus et futuris"*) and which seems to destroy any alternative and ascribe a necessity to all things' (*Cur Deus Homo*, II, XVIII(a), p. 277), is contrasted with antecedent necessity thus:

> ...when the heavens are said to revolve, it is an antecedent and efficient necessity, for they must revolve. But when I say that you speak of necessity, because you are speaking, this is nothing but a subsequent and imperative necessity. For I mean only that it is impossible for you to speak and not to speak at the same time, and not that someone compels you to speak. For the force of its own nature makes the heaven revolve; but no necessity obliges you to speak.   —ibid., pp. 276—7

I am not here concerned with whether or not this is a particularly happy use of the term 'necessity', noting simply that D. P. Henry considers that there are good grounds for interpreting Anselm's 'subsequent necessity' as an exemplification of 'the logical thesis to the effect that (where "p" is a propositional variable) for all p, if p then p...'.[3] If this is indeed the case, and it is consistent with Anselm's view that 'wherever there is an antecedent necessity, there is also a subsequent one; but not vice-versa' (p. 277), then the concluding clause of the statement 'Necessarily, if God exists, then God exists', is necessarily true only if God actually exists. What matters is that Anselm's 'subsequent necessity' cannot be used to conclude that God exists from the fact that 'God exists' is a necessarily true proposition (if it is) because *this* necessity attaches not to the proposition 'God exists', but to the proposition 'If God exists, then God exists'.

> By this subsequent and imperative necessity was it necessary (since the belief and prophecy concerning Christ were true, that he would die of his own free will) that it should be so.
> —ibid., p. 277

It seems that all Anselm is saying here is that it is necessarily the case that if it is true that p, then p; for if p did not follow, a contradiction would arise. If it is true that God exists, then, necessarily, he exists, just as, if it is true that Anselm said such-and-such, then, necessarily, he said it. The appropriateness of Anselm's calling this a *necessary* state of affairs is not here at issue. What is important is to see that the sense in which God exists of necessity, in the present sense of 'subsequent necessity', if he exists, or if it is true that he exists, is quite different from the sense in which propositions like 'Triangles have three sides', or 'Some squares are circular' are necessary propositions. There is nothing remarkable or special or unique about the concept of God which entails his necessarily existing, for 'If x exists, then of necessity, x exists' is true for *any* value of x: 'This subsequent necessity pertains to everything...' (ibid.). Quite clearly this is not the same notion of necessity as that in contemporary modal logic; Anselm's insistence that subsequent necessity pertains to everything is sufficient to show that.

Common in Anselm, especially in the *Monologion*, is the idea of inferential necessity.[4] A conclusion is said to be necessary, because, if one is reasoning validly, only it and no other conclusion is obtainable from the premises given. Such a conclusion need not of course be necessarily true. Rather, the necessity resides in our being forced to the conclusion by rational argument:

> Therefore the rational existence of the truth must first be shown, I mean, the necessity, which proves that God ought to or could have, condescended to do those things we affirm.
> —*Cur Deus Homo*, I, IV, p. 184
> How, then, shall these propositions, that are so necessary according to our exposition, and so necessary according to our proof, be reconciled?[5]
> —*Monologion*, XXII, p. 78

If it is true that the programme at the Odeon changes every Sunday, and tomorrow is Sunday, then, of necessity, the programme at the Odeon will change tomorrow; or, the programme will necessarily change tomorrow. Clearly, however, 'The programme will change tomorrow' is not a necessary proposition.

Of the ways in which Anselm uses the concept, or concepts, of necessity in *Cur Deus Homo* and the *Monologion*, then, none corresponds to logical necessity. If, as Hartshorne and Malcolm think, Anselm does use the alleged logical necessity of 'God exists' as the basic premiss in a proof of God's existence in *Proslogion* III and the *Reply*, then his use of that notion — so far as works to do specifically with God, his attributes, and his relation to man, are concerned — is peculiar to the *Proslogion* and *Reply*. And even if that were in fact the case, we would still be left with the unpromising task of accounting for the total absence from *Cur Deus Homo* (probably written between 1094 and 1098) of a crucial idea, an idea introduced some twenty years earlier in the *Proslogion* and *Reply*, from which, allegedly, God's existence may be deduced. Most importantly, we should have to account for its absence from ch. XVIII(a) of Bk. II, where Anselm specifically discusses 'How, with God there is neither necessity nor impossibility...' (p. 273).

Turning to the *Proslogion*, we find in the title of ch. XXIII, 'necessary' applied not to arguments or states of affairs, but to a being:

> That this good is equally Father and Son and Holy Spirit; and that this is the one necessary being which is altogether and wholly and solely good. —p. 145

This might at first be thought odd, since it suggests that there are *a number* of necessary beings, of which only one is wholly good. If Anselm has earlier, in ch. III, singled out the necessity of God's existence as being unique to God, why does he now deny just that? He certainly seems to do so, concluding the chapter thus:

> 'Moreover, one thing is necessary.' [Luke, X, 42] This is, moreover, that one thing necessary in which is every good, or rather, which is wholly and uniquely and completely and solely good.
> —p. 147

The first sentence[6] suggests one necessary being; but the comment again suggests several. There may be a confusion in this passage between 'necessary' in the sense of 'needful', 'needed by us' (God is the only thing we really do need, according to the biblical quotation) and 'necessary' in some other sense. For in his comment on the quotation, Anselm appears to be saying — as in the title of the chapter — that *this* necessary thing is different from all other necessary things because it is wholly good. Although it is possible to read Anselm's 'necessary' in the same way as in his quotation, without the suggestion of several necessary things — but at the cost of reading it other than in the chapter's title — I think the proposed reading better. For it is clear, as I shall show, that Anselm does not take God's unique status to reside in his necessity.

As this is the only passage in the *Proslogion* where Anselm uses 'necessary' of God, it would seem that the way in which he is said to be necessary here accords, or fails to accord, with Anselm's ascription to us, in ch. III, of an inability even to think that God does not exist, ought to shed light on the question of whether or not ch. III is a proof of God's existence based on the idea of his logically necessary status. The reading proposed, however, suggests that Hartshorne's characterization of Anselm's Principle as 'perfection could not exist contingently'[7] (quite apart from my earlier objections to the idea of perfection) is mistaken. For, if perfection (i.e., God) is not thought to be *unique* in existing necessarily, then any proof of God's existence based on this sense of 'necessary existence' could equally well be used to prove the existence of all or any of those other beings whose existence is treated as necessary. But if that were indeed the case, why does Anselm not seek to prove that God exists in a similar way to that in which he would seek to prove that other necessary beings exist? Why go to all the trouble of trying to prove, in ch. III, not that God 'necessarily exists', but that 'something than which a greater cannot be conceived so truly is that it is impossible to conceive of it as not existing'?

The simple point is that Anselm actually distinguishes God from other necessary beings, and not, as Hartshorne thinks, God from other beings on account of his necessary status. Unlike anything else, *necessary or not*, God exists 'so truly that he cannot be thought not to exist'. If God's existence did follow from his necessary status, in Anselm's sense of 'necessary', then the existence of everything which has this necessary status would also follow from it. But this is not the case: 'The salient point, and one which is totally overlooked by most moderns, is that beings which are necessary (i.e., not possible not to be) are, according to the Boethian cosmological background of the commentaries from which Anselm draws his modal logic, comparatively commonplace. One has only to look up into the night sky to see evidence of many such beings. The heavenly bodies provide Boethius with a set of standard examples of necessary beings.'[8] But the heavenly bodies, although they exist, and are necessary, *can* be imagined not to exist. If, however, their existence were to follow from their status as necessary beings, they could not be imagined not to exist; since, if one were to imagine a star as not existing, it would not in fact be the star one was actually imagining, because one cannot imagine something as not existing which is *unable* not to exist. Unlike God however, stars are not unable not to exist. That, at least, is Anselm's doctrine. He does not ask the crucial question as to the modal status of a proposition such as 'God is unable not to exist', since the modern distinction between necessary and contingent propositions was not available to him. Nowhere to my knowledge does he elaborate on the nature of this inability on the part of God. Clearly, however, this is a crucial issue, which I shall treat in ch. 5. My concern here is only with what is and what is not attributable to Anselm. For the time being, then, the reader must make do with 'unable' *tout court*. As far as Anselm is concerned, if we know that something is unable not to exist, we cannot imagine *it* as not existing, just as we cannot imagine a triangle as not having three sides. But, whereas in the case of triangles we cannot imagine them as other than three-sided because it is *a matter of logic* that they have three sides — anything not three-sided, is, as a matter of logic, not a triangle —Anselm's reasons for supposing that we cannot imagine God as not existing because he is unable not to exist, are rather different. What these are I shall discuss later (p. 32ff.). The important exegetical point here is that according to Anselm, God is to be distinguished from all other beings in that he cannot be imagined not to exist. But he does not call *that* feature of God his necessity, since 'to prove that God was a necessary being, or that God necessarily existed, would scarcely be a way of exalting God above his creation'.[9] In Anselm, 'x cannot be thought not to exist' is emphatically not equivalent to '"x exists" is necessarily true'.

In Anselm's *Reply*, it is inferential necessity which is prominent, although it is often far from clear that this is in fact the notion present. Indeed, this unclarity may have been instrumental in misleading Hartshorne.[10] One example will be sufficient to show this:

> I insist, however, that simply if it can be thought to exist[11] it is necessary that it exists in reality. For 'that than which a greater cannot be thought' cannot be thought save as being without a beginning. But whatever can be thought as existing and does not actually exist, can be thought as having a beginning of its existence. Consequently, 'that than which a greater cannot be thought' cannot be thought as existing and yet not actually exist. If, therefore, it can be thought as existing, it exists of necessity.
> —*Reply*, I, pp. 169—171

This passage is one of those that Hartshorne takes to be part of the set of arguments used by Anselm to establish the logical necessity of God's existence: indeed, it is central to his thesis.[12] While an analysis of this passage in terms of logical necessity is clearly possible, it is equally clearly out of place as an analysis of an C11th. text.

Anselm simply did not posses the modern notion of logical necessity: inferential necessity and propositional necessity are quite different. But since this matter has engendered so much confusion, it may be as well to consider the following example.

(1) Bananas are yellow.
(2) 'Being yellow' entails 'being coloured'.
(3) Therefore, bananas are coloured.

Anselm might say, for (3), 'Therefore, bananas are necessarily coloured'. But 'bananas are coloured' is certainly not a logically necessary proposition. It merely follows necessarily from (1) and (2). Bananas, being yellow, cannot but be coloured, given the truth of (1) and (2); and, if we follow the argument correctly, we cannot but come to the conclusion, (3). Now compare the following argument:

(1a) God is that than which nothing greater can be thought.
(2a) 'That than which nothing greater can be thought' entails 'existing'.
(3a) Therefore, God exists.

(3a) follows necessarily from (1a) and (2a). God, being that than which nothing greater can be thought, cannot but exist, given the truth of (1a) and (2a); and, if we follow the argument correctly, we cannot but come to the conclusion, (3a). This is no modal argument. In fact, it is Anselm's argument in *Proslogion* II! (It does of course differ in at least one crucial respect from the argument about bananas. One can imagine colourless bananas, I think, and still be imagining bananas, because it is not the case that nothing which is not yellow can be a banana. One cannot, however, imagine God as non-existent, and still be imagining God, because it is the case — by definition — that nothing which is not that than which nothing greater can be thought can be God.)

Now, the argument in *Reply* I may be stated as follows, with 'T' for 'that than which nothing greater can be thought':
(1) T 'cannot be thought save as being without a beginning', since
(2) anything that exists and has never not existed is greater than anything that exists but has at some time not existed.[13]
(3) But any non-existent entity, which can nevertheless be conceived to exist, must be conceived as having a beginning. Therefore
(4) T cannot be a non-existent entity which can be conceived to exist. Thus
(5) if T is an entity which can be conceived to exist, then T cannot be a non-existent entity. Therefore
(6) T must exist if it can be conceived to exist.

Now this is certainly a separate argument for the existence of God: but Anselm's conclusion, that if T 'can be thought as existing, it exists of necessity', does not bring in the notion of logical necessity. Anselm is simply saying that the conclusion follows 'of necessity': this is another example of inferential necessity. The reason for Anselm why T must exist if it can be conceived to exist, is not that T's existence is a matter of logical necessity, but that T cannot be a non-existent but conceivable entity, since such entities have a beginning; but T cannot, by definition, have a beginning. So if T is a conceivable entity, it must be an existent and not a non-existent, entity. Hartshorne is misled because the entities referred to in (3) are in fact what we would call logically possible entities — entities which can be conceived of as existing but which do not in fact exist. Certainly, Anselm contrasts T with such entities: but it is not their modal status, but rather the fact that T 'cannot be thought save as without a beginning', which he contrasts with the fact that the other entities in question can be so conceived. Now, it may or may not be the case that if T is without a beginning,

27

i.e. if T is eternal, then 'T exists' must be a necessary proposition (see ch. 5): but whether this is so is a separate issue from that under discussion here. What *Anselm* is concerned to do in this passage is to show that, since God cannot be a member of the class of entities which may begin to exist, he cannot be a member of the class of fictions: for the two classes are mutually exclusive. Certainly, it may be the case that Anselm's idea of supreme greatness contains that of eternal existence, in which case, given that God is by definition supremely great, it follows that it is necessarily true that he is eternal. And it may furthermore be the case that an eternal being exists necessarily, in that the proposition asserting his existence must be a necessary proposition, as Hartshorne and Malcolm maintain. Anselm's argument, however, does not rest on *this*, but rather on his principle that eternal existence is greater than temporal existence. If God's existence is logically necessary, an issue with which Anselm was not concerned, then that this is so is quite distinct from the fact that God's existence follows necessarily from certain premises.

Similar considerations apply to the second argument in *Reply* I, on which Malcolm hangs so much in 'Anselm's Ontological Arguments': 'necessarily' in Anselm's statement of the thesis, 'even if it can be thought of, then certainly it necessarily exists' (p. 171), refers to the unavoidability of the conclusion. Here, in fact, there may be some doubt as to whether it is inferential necessity or coercive antecedent necessity which Anselm has in mind. But the latter would suggest that our ability to think of God in some way coerces him; and this runs counter to Anselm's other statements on the matter, and indeed counter to his view that what is the case causes the truth of statements.[14] Furthermore, the third argument of what is clearly a trio of arguments of a similar form in *Reply* I makes no mention of necessity; it claims simply that God 'exists as a whole at every time and in every place' (p. 173), because anything which does not so exist can be thought not to exist, and this is not true of God. In fact, the statement of this tells quite conclusively against Hartshorne's and Malcolm's interpretation of Anselm: 'But "that than which a greater cannot be thought" cannot be thought not to exist *if it does actually exist*...' (p. 173, my italics). Surely this shows that Anselm does not mean by 'cannot be thought not to exist' what Hartshorne and

Malcolm mean by 'exists necessarily'; for the factual condition, 'if it does actually exist', cannot state the condition for the truth of a necessary proposition, whereas it can and does state the condition for the truth of Anselm's claim that '(it) cannot be thought not to exist'. The movement of Anselm's thought is the exact reverse of that in modal logic, namely from what is in fact the case to what can be thought, and not from what can be thought to what is necessarily the case.

In *Reply* I, Anselm elaborates on the implications of God's being 'that than which nothing greater can be thought': and he gives two arguments to God's existence based on the formula's being understood. Rather than treating the passage as an elaboration of *Proslogion* III, therefore, as Hartshorne and Malcolm take it, it would be better to regard it as an elaboration of *Proslogion* II, the argument of which is based on just the same point. Certainly, to treat the two arguments to God's existence in *Reply* I as arguments from the necessary truth of the proposition 'God exists' is altogether wrong. I do not of course deny that the passage has modal implications, and that these are central to an assessment of Anselm's argument — indeed I shall argue to this effect in ch. 5. But there is no modal argument in Anselm's *Reply*.

We may now turn to *Proslogion* III, and the claim that God 'cannot be thought not to exist'. Hartshorne regards this chapter as stating the fundamental point of Anselm's argument, that, in the case of God, '"existence" is not a mere question of fact, but of logical necessity'.[15] But, whether or not it turns out to be the case that God's existence is a matter of logical necessity, and whether or not this turns out to be *in fact* the essential point of Anselm's argument, the question of what *Anselm* considered essential is another matter. The essential point *in fact* and the essential point *intended* need not, after all, be one and the same. Anselm's arguments in *Proslogion* III are more complex and circuitous than Hartshorne takes them to be. And the intended conclusion is not at all what Hartshorne takes it to be.

Of the two arguments in the chapter, the second is an elaboration of the first, and a reiteration of its premiss on the basis of its conclusion. The first may be set out as follows:

(1) We can conceive of something such that its non-existence is inconceivable.

(2) This is greater than anything, the non-existence of

which is conceivable.
(3) If the non-existence of that than which nothing greater can be thought were conceivable, then it would not be that than which nothing greater can be thought,
(4) since the entity referred to in (1) would be greater than it (from (2)).
(5) But that than which nothing greater can be thought cannot not be that than which nothing greater can be thought.
(6) Therefore that than which nothing greater can be thought is such that its non-existence is inconceivable.

If Anselm does not mean by (in my words) 'its non-existence is inconceivable' that its existence is logically necessary, then what does he mean? How is the argument to be understood?

In *Reply* IV, Anselm refers to 'the distinguishing characteristic of God [as] not to be able to be understood not to exist' (p. 177). Whereas 'many things, the while they do exist, cannot be thought of as not existing' (in the sense that, if we know a thing exists, we cannot at the same time think it does not exist; but *not* in the sense that we cannot *imagine* that it does not exist), 'it is the distinguishing characteristic of God that He cannot be thought of as not existing' (p. 179) (in *both* senses). This brings out clearly the point that Anselm regards God's inability to be thought not to exist as one of his attributes: and *Reply* III makes it clear that God's inability to be thought not to exist follows from his inability not to be:

> It has already been clearly seen, however, that 'that than which a greater cannot be thought' cannot be thought not to exist, because it exists as a matter of such certain truth...[16]   —p. 175

For Anselm, God's inability not to exist logically precedes his inability to be thought not to exist. The movement is from what *is* the case, to what can truly be thought to be the case; whereas on Hartshorne's interpretation, the movement is from what is, or can be, thought to be the case, to what actually is the case, from a necessarily true proposition about God, to God's existence.

I am now in a position to re-examine *Proslogion* III. The first argument, outlined above, shows that God is unable to be thought not to exist, because, if this were not the case, he would not be that than which nothing greater can be thought. The argument is a *reductio*, of which an exactly similar form could be used to show that God had *any* property, to have which renders him greater than he would be were he not to have it. That in this particular case the property should be the inability to be thought not to exist is of no special consequence. We know, therefore, that we are conceiving of God correctly, only if we conceive of him as existing; and we know this, because to do otherwise engenders a contradiction. But why is something, the non-existence of which is inconceivable, greater than anything, the non-existence of which is not inconceivable? I discussed earlier Anselm's grounds for holding that existents have a higher ontological status than non-existents. But what are his grounds for holding that entities with the attribute of being unable to be thought not to exist have a higher ontological status than entities lacking this attribute? He maintains that our inability to think of God as non-existent is a consequence of his existing 'so truly' that he cannot be thought not to exist. It is thus *evidence* that God exists in such a manner that he cannot not exist — that is, that he exists in the highest degree. Being unable to be thought not to exist is a consequence of existing in the highest degree; therefore, if discovered, it is evidence of the latter. But it has been discovered, inasmuch as its putative absence has been shown to engender a contradiction. We thus have evidence that God exists in the highest degree.

This is what Anselm spells out in the second of his arguments in *Proslogion* III:
(1) 'You exist so truly, Lord my God, that You cannot even be thought not to exist.' Since
(2) You are indeed that than which nothing greater can be thought (and thus exist in the highest degree, as was shown in ch. II); and since
(3) 'everything else there is, except You alone, can be thought of as not existing'.

(2) eliminates the possibility of God's not existing in the highest degree in one way, by showing that a denial of (2) is a contradiction ('...the creature would be above its creator and would judge its creator — and that is completely absurd'). (3) reinforces that conclusion by reminding us that, since everything except God can be thought of as not existing,

everything which exists, exists in a lesser degree than God; for what we are able to think regarding the ability of something to exist or not to exist is evidence of that ability. This argument, in particular (3) above, explains the assumption made in the first argument in the chapter that something which cannot be thought not to exist is greater than something which can be thought not to exist.[17] The *suppressed* assumption in all this, however, is an instance of Anselm's epistemological principle that what is the case causes the truth of the statement that it is the case. As McGill says, Anselm holds that '...whenever we conceive of something that does exist but might not exist, that thing always shows the possibility of its non-existence to our minds...["that than which a greater cannot be conceived"] does not show any possibility of its non-existence to our minds...(so) there is objectively within it no possibility of its non-existence'.[18] That God cannot be thought not to exist is proved by a *reductio*: the grounds for that *reductio* are the conclusion of *Proslogion* II, that God exists, and Anselm's epistemological principle. Our inability to think that God does not exist, if it is truly God we have in mind, is a peculiar property *of God*, because it depends on *his* inability not to exist; our inability is *evidence* of God's inability insofar as it is an attribute of God which is evident to us, and which can be evident to us only if God is indeed unable not to exist. However problematic this may be, and Anselm fails to give detailed grounds for his position in the *Proslogion*, *Reply*, *Monologion*, or *Cur Deus Homo*,[19] what emerges clearly is that the movement of Anselm's thought in *Proslogion* III is not, as Hartshorne and Malcolm would have it, from any logical necessity of God's existence to his existing, but the very opposite: 'It is evident, then, that it [that than which nothing greater can be thought] neither does not exist, nor can not exist, or be thought of as not existing' (*Reply* V, p. 181). That God does exist is the conclusion of *Proslogion* II; that he cannot be thought not to exist the conclusion, derived from his being unable not to exist, of *Proslogion* III.

I have argued that in claiming that God is unable not to exist, Anselm is not to be understood as claiming that 'God exists' is a necessarily true proposition. What exactly, then, does he mean by the claim? In ch. XIII of the *Proslogion* Anselm writes:

> All that which is enclosed in any way by place or time is less than that which no law of place or time constrains. Since, then, nothing is greater than You, no place or time confines You but You exist everywhere and always. And because this can be said of You alone, You alone are unlimited and eternal... You alone are said to be eternal because, alone of all beings, You will not cease to exist just as You have not begun to exist. —p. 133

And he goes on to say:

> You were not, therefore, yesterday, not will You be tomorrow, but yesterday and today and tomorrow You *are*. Indeed You exist neither yesterday nor today nor tomorrow but are absolutely outside all time. For yesterday and today and tomorrow are completely in time; however, You, though nothing can be without You, are nevertheless not in place or time but all things are in You. —ch. XIX, pp. 141–143

This is to say that God is eternal and self-sufficient; and Anselm deduces this on the basis of his original formula, that God is that than which nothing greater can be thought. 'For "that than which a greater cannot be thought" cannot be thought save as being without a beginning' (*Reply* I, pp. 169); '...that which does not have an end in any way at all is beyond that which does come to an end in some way' (*Pros.* XX, p. 143). That being which is 'completely sufficient unto (Himself), needing nothing, but rather He whom all things need in order that they may have being and well-being' (*Pros.* XXII, p. 145) is the most real possible being. The form of the argument is this: if x is (or does) p, then x is not a; but x is a; therefore x cannot be (or do) p. God cannot not exist because he is eternal and self-sufficient.

A good exposition of the relation between God's self-sufficiency and his timelessness is given by Anselm himself in the *Monologion*. There he does not derive these truths about God from the definition of him as that than which nothing greater can be thought. Rather, the movement is the other way. God, since he is a self-sufficient being, most truly exists: '...that which exists through itself exists in the greatest degree of all things' (ch. III, p. 42). Having concluded that there is indeed a being through whom everything there is has its being, Anselm continues: 'Since, then, all things that are exist through this one being, doubtless this one being exists through itself' (ibid.) and 'this Nature derives existence from itself, but other beings from it' (ch. V, p. 46). He explains this as follows:

> Since it is evident, then, that this Nature is whatever it is, through itself, and all other beings are what they are, through it, how does it exist through itself? For, what is said to exist through anything apparently exists through an efficient agent, or through matter, or through some external aid, as through some instrument. But, whatever exists in any of these three ways exists through another than itself, and it is of later existence, and, in some sort, less than that through which it obtains existence.
> But, in no wise does the supreme Nature exist through another, nor is it later or less than itself or anything else. Therefore, the supreme Nature could be created neither by itself, nor by another; nor could itself or any other be the matter whence it should be created; nor did it assist itself in any way; nor did anything assist it to be what it was not before. —ch. VI, pp. 46—7

From this, it follows that God is eternal:

> But it is certain, according to truths already made plain, that in no wise does it derive existence from another, or from nothing [since nothing can derive existence from nothing];...Moreover, it cannot have inception from or through itself, although it exists from and through itself. For it so exists from and through itself, that by no means is there one essence which exists from and through itself, and another through which, and from which, it exists. But, whatever begins to exist from or through something, is by no means identical with that from or through which it begins to exist. Therefore, the supreme Nature does not begin through or from itself.
> Seeing, then, that it has a beginning neither through nor from itself, and neither through nor from nothing, it assuredly has no beginning at all. But neither will it have an end. For, if it is to have an end, it is not supremely immortal and supremely incorruptible. But we have proved that it is supremely immortal and supremely incorruptible. Therefore, it will not have an end.
> Furthermore, if it is to have an end, it will perish either willingly or against its will. But certainly that is not a simple, unmixed good, at whose will the supreme good perishes. But this being is itself the true and simple, unmixed good. Therefore, that very being, which is certainly the supreme good, will not die of its own will. If, however, it is to perish against its will, it is not supremely powerful, or all-powerful. But cogent reasoning has asserted it to be powerful and all-powerful. Therefore, it will not die against its will. Hence, if neither with nor against its will the supreme Nature is to have an end, in no way will it have an end.
> —ch. XVIII, pp. 68—9

An eternal being, then, cannot derive its existence from anything, since if it did, it would either have begun to exist, and thus it would not be eternal, or it would be self-caused, which Anselm regards as incoherent, since if a causes b, a and b cannot be identical. Nor can it be dependent for its continuing existence on anything other than itself, since it would then be possible that it should cease to exist, and thus not be eternal. Nor, if it is self-sufficient, can its existence come to an end, since, if its existence came to an end of its own volition, it would not be what it is — eternal — and if its existence were brought to an end by something other than itself, it would not be self-sufficient.

I shall analyse this in detail in ch. 5, particularly the modal status of God's inability not to exist, and thus the question of the modal status of the existence of an eternal and self-sufficient being. It is clear, however, that these questions do not arise in Anselm's own work; and therefore that, contrary to Hartshorne and Malcolm, ch. III of the *Proslogion* is not the repository of Anselm's argument for the existence of God.[20]

Chapter

Proslogion II

Having discussed Anselm's metaphysical background, I am in a position to examine in detail the argument of *Proslogion* II. It may be set out as follows:

(1) '...We believe that You are something than which nothing greater can be thought'.
(2) 'Something than which nothing greater can be thought' is understood, and
(3) it therefore exists 'in the mind'.
(4) Assume that that than which a greater cannot be thought exists in the mind alone; then
(5) that than which a greater cannot be thought can be conceived to exist in reality.
(6) To exist in reality and in the mind is greater than to exist in the mind alone.
(7) Therefore (4,5,6) something can be conceived to be greater than that than which a greater cannot be thought;
(8) 'But this is obviously impossible.'
(9) 'Therefore there is absolutely no doubt that something than which a greater cannot be thought exists both in the mind and in reality.'

I shall refer to step (1) as Anselm's formula. The questions which arise in connection with its role in the argument are central for any interpretation: the various forms it takes relate directly to the question of whether it is a definition or a description; this in turn is bound up with that of the role of the Fool and the whole nature of the argument, whether rationalistic or fideistic; and finally the intelligibility of the formula can be properly estimated only in the light of discussion of these problems. The major part of this chapter, then, will be concerned with Anselm's formula, following the order outlined above.

Anselm's formula takes the following forms in the *Proslogion* and *Reply*:
- (a) something than which nothing greater can be thought
  (aliquid quo nihil maius cogitari possit)
- (b) that than which a greater cannot be thought
  (id quo maius cogitari nequit/non potest/non possit)
- (c) something than which a greater cannot be thought
  (aliquid quo maius cogitari non valet/potest/possit)
- (d) that than which nothing greater can be thought
  (id quo maius cogitari non potest)

(a), (b), and (c) occur, in that order, in *Proslogion* II: (b) and (c) in *Proslogion* III: (d) in *Proslogion* IV. In the *Reply*, (b) is by far the most common, but (c) also occurs occasionally. I do not think that anything crucial hangs on these variations as they occur in the text, since Anselm appears to use them interchangeably.[1] One of the variations, however, may help make clearer just what Anselm has in mind. For 'God is something than which...' ((a) and (c)) might appear to suggest a description of God: 'God is that than which...' ((b) and (d)) a definition. But it is clear from (1) — (9) above that Anselm himself does not differentiate between 'something than...' and 'that than...'. Further, God is said to be that/something than which *nothing* greater can be thought only at the beginning of ch. II, and in chs. IV and V. Otherwise the formula is 'that/something than which *a* greater cannot be thought'. If God is that/something than which nothing greater can be thought, it follows that he is that/something than which a greater cannot be thought, but not vice-versa. He could be the being than which *a greater being* cannot be thought without being that/something than which *nothing* greater can be thought. '...than which a...' carries with it a suggestion of God as *a being* which is absent from '...than which nothing...'. One might speculate, fancifully perhaps, as to whether or not Anselm might have sensed this, and therefore used '...than which nothing...' at the beginning of the argument in order to escape the charge of prejudging the nature of God, but then slipped into '...than which a...'. However this may be, since the formula employing 'nothing' suggests a reference to an ontologically supreme entity somewhat more strongly than that employing 'a' (*nothing greater can be conceived*, and not just *a greater being* cannot be conceived) I shall adopt the former variant throughout, except when quoting directly from Anselm.

As I have suggested that 'something than which nothing greater can be thought' may more aptly be taken as a description, and 'that than which nothing greater can be thought' as a definition, this will be an appropriate place to consider the nature of Anselm's formula. It is generally assumed to be a definition: Barth, however, takes it to be a 'revealed Name of God';[2] La Croix objects to the general assumption because he wishes to maintain that Anselm's subject in chs. II and III is not God, but 'that than which nothing greater can be thought';[3] and Richard Campbell takes a similar line, arguing that Anselm employs the formula to identify God.[4] Just what status of term Barth takes 'a revealed Name of God' to be is quite unclear; certainly he presents no argument that the formula is not a definition, and his characterization of it seems simply to serve his general view of the argument as an expression of faith rather than as a serious attempt to convince the Fool that he is wrong. Nor does La Croix make any suggestion as to what the formula is, if not a definition; and apart from the fact that its being a definition does not fit in with his exceedingly odd interpretation of the argument,[5] his objection is that as a definition, the formula has no religious significance. But this amounts to no more than a stipulation that Greek metaphysics is irrelevant to Christianity. It is in fact just because the formula is acceptable to the Fool on the basis of the platonism he shares with him that Anselm chooses it. He then proceeds to show the Fool the religious significance of what he already accepts to be the case. The point is that the Fool can understand the formula 'in some way [whereas] he would understand ... ["God"] ... in no way at all' (*Reply* VII, p. 185). Campbell, however, cites this passage from *Reply* VII as 'quite conclusive evidence' for his insistence that Anselm does not regard his formula as a definition, an interpretation central to his neo-Wittgensteinian reading of Anselm.[6] He comments on Anselm's remark that '...it cannot be believed that anyone should deny "that than which a greater cannot be thought" (which, being heard, he understands to some extent), on the ground that he denies

God whose meaning he does not think of in any way at all' (ibid.) that it shows that he does not 'take "that-than-which-a-greater-cannot-be-thought" to mean the same as "God", since one can understand the former but not the latter'.[7] Having misjudged the role of the Fool in the argument as an incidental one, Campbell cannot but miss the point of Anselm's procedure here. For what he is doing is to bring to the notice of Gaunilo, the Fool, and any other potential apologist for the latter, that in assenting to p of 'that than which nothing greater can be thought', one is logically committed to assenting to p of 'God'. If a proposition is acknowledged to be true of, for example, 'eight children born of a single pregnancy', then logical consistency demands that it be acknowledged to be true of 'octuplets'. Anselm is showing the Fool that, since 'eight children born of a single pregnancy', a phrase understood by both of them, is a definition of 'octuplets', then inasmuch as the Fool must admit p of the former (must admit, if the argument of *Proslogion* II is sound, that that than which nothing greater can be thought exists), he is committed to acknowledging p of the latter, even though he does not, initially, understand the term. In fact, Campbell's insistence that the formula is an 'identification' of God merely obscures the issue. What could an identification consist in, other than either an identifying description or a definition?

There are however two other objections against taking the formula as a definition. First, and most important, is that if it is a definition then its subject, 'God', cannot be a proper name — and Anselm is clearly using 'God' as a proper name in much of the *Proslogion*. I shall discuss this question in ch. 5. For the moment I simply note that if, as I argue below, the formula is a definition, then what it defines cannot of course be either a proper name or its bearer. To insist as Campbell does, however, that the formula cannot be a definition just because Anselm uses 'God' as a proper name will not do — especially as logically varied use of 'God' is a striking feature of the Christian tradition. Second, the formula tells us something about what can be thought, rather than about its purported definiendum: if it is a definition, then it would seem to be a singularly indirect one. If we recall however, that for Anselm our inability to think that something is or is not the case is due to a necessity or impossibility *de re* regarding the subject of our thought, then it is clear that his formula is, in his eyes at least, a logical consequence of God's manner of existing. God is that than which nothing more real can be thought because God is that than which there can be nothing more real. That is why 'God' may be taken as a synonym for 'that than which nothing greater can be thought'.[8]

Furthermore, it is because God is that than which there can be nothing more real that he is 'also something greater than can be thought...since it is possible to think that there is such a one' (*Pros.* XV, p. 137). The point Anselm is making here is that God is that than which nothing greater can be thought because he is that than which there can be nothing greater; but is nevertheless also greater than can be thought, i.e., is more real than we can fully conceive. For Campbell, 'it is hard to understand this twist to the dialectic'[9] if Anselm's formula is taken as a definition: but whereas 'God is that than which nothing greater can be thought' may properly be read as 'God is that than which nothing more real is possible', 'God is something greater than can be thought' cannot properly be read as 'God is something more real than is possible'. And this is precisely because the first is a definition, setting logical limits to its definiendum, and the second merely a description. In the first, what 'can be thought' is identical with what 'is possible' because the phrase tells us something about God. In the second, 'what can be thought' tells us something about *our thought* in relation to God. 'No mountain higher than Mt. Everest can be thought' is clearly not identical to 'No mountain higher than Mt. Everest is possible'. The former, whether true or false, describes our thought in relation to Mt. Everest, whereas the latter states something (false) about Mt. Everest. 'No mountain higher than Mt. Everest is possible' is nonsense (just the same sort of nonsense as 'No island more perfect than the Lost Island is possible') because mountains cannot be defined — whereas our thinking about them, just like our thinking about that than which nothing more real can be thought, can be described. Campbell simply fails to distinguish how 'can be thought' functions in a definition from how it functions in a description.[10]

If the formula were not a definition, then presumably it would be a description. Consideration of the relative merits of taking it as one or the other confirms that it is to be taken as a definition, and strongly suggests that this was Anselm's intention, although he nowhere explicitly says so. If God were being described as that than which nothing greater can be thought, the Fool might well ask what leads Anselm to suppose the description to be accurate. For it would be accurate only if God actually existed: since all existents are greater than any non-existent, and given that something exists, God may be described as the greatest possible entity only if he exists. A description does not entail that there *is* anything which is being described, since the description may simply fail to have application. The Fool could argue very reasonably on the basis of his belief that there is no God, that a description which entails that God does exist cannot be true of him. If the formula is a definition, however, then criticism of Anselm on the basis of alleged question-begging is misplaced. For given that the definition is coherent — and this Anselm assumes illegitimately, as I shall argue later, but carrying the Fool with him — then there *is* something which is the definiendum. For if coherent, then a definition defines *something*, whatever its ontological status may be. There is no question of having to "locate" the definiendum to check the definition against it. Even if what is defined is only an idea, nevertheless, the articulation of the definition, since it is a complete statement of what the idea in question is, is at once the articulation of the definiendum. A description, however, since it is an incomplete statement of what something is, cannot function in this way. It is on this basis that Anselm carries the Fool with him. If the Fool understands the formula, and 'obviously if it is spoken of in a known language and he does not understand it, then either he has no intelligence at all, or a completely obtuse one' (*Reply* II, p. 173), then he cannot without contradiction hold that it has no subject. This is central to a proper understanding of the argument. It is because the formula is a definition that it can be the means of seeking to convince the Fool. Were it a description, then its truly describing anything, let alone God, would be in question, even if the Fool understood it; but once the Fool admits to the coherence of a definition, then there can be no question of its not truly defining *something* — though not necessarily, of course, something which exists. What is more, a definition is the definition of one sort or class of thing only, whereas a description may describe all sorts of things: that it individuates in this way is what makes something a definition rather than just a description. And of course Anselm wants his formula to pick out one sort of thing only, which is just what it could not do were it a description.

Much of the foregoing depends on the role one ascribes to the Fool in *Proslogion* II – IV. The greater the extent to which the argument is understood in fideistic terms, the less emphasis will be placed on Anselm's attempt to show the Fool the inconsistency of his position: Stolz, Barth, and La Croix, for example, deny that this is any part of Anselm's intention at all, while Campbell thinks that he 'remembers the fool after he has arrived at his first two conclusions concerning God only to muse on the question of how the fool could ever have said what he did'.[11] Such a view of course relegates considerations of the assumedly shared metaphysics of Anselm and the Fool to a very minor part, thereby naturally veering away from regarding the formula as the agreed definition exemplifying this shared basis. This is what Anselm says in explanation of 'How "the Fool said in his heart" what cannot be thought':

> For in one sense a thing is thought [cogitatur] when the word signifying it is thought [cogitatur]; in another sense when the very object which the thing is is understood [intelligitur]. In the first sense, then, God can be thought [cogitari] not to exist, but not at all in the second sense. —*Proslogion* IV, pp. 119–121

Far from relegating his concern with the Fool to a secondary place, he devotes nearly all of *Proslogion* IV to explaining how it is that the Fool could have been brought to see the implications of what he already assented to, namely that God is that than which nothing greater can be thought. For whereas the Fool could refer to 'God' but misconceive (cogitare) the nature of its referent – simply get God wrong – he cannot properly understand (intelligere) the term without understanding (intelligere) the nature of its referent, understanding, that is, that its nature is such that it must exist. Anselm is here, although not consistently in the *Reply*, using 'cogitare' as we might use 'conceive', and 'intelligere' as we might use 'understand', or better, 'conceive correctly'.[12] The Fool has been shown the implications of conceiving correctly something to which he already gives assent. If anything more is needed to make this clear, then consider Anselm's concluding sentence in ch. IV: 'I give thanks, good Lord, I give thanks to You, since what I believed before through Your free gift I now so understand through Your illumination, that if I did not want *to believe* that You existed, I should nevertheless be unable not to *understand* [intelligere] it.' Even if he were a Fool, and did not want to believe that there was a God, Anselm should nonetheless have been forced to concede that there was a God, having been brought by the argument to a proper understanding of 'God'. Anselm expressly says of his *Reply* to Gaunilo that it is directed against *the Christian*, and not the Fool 'against whom I spoke *in my tract*' (preface to *Reply*, p. 169, my italics). The point made by Campbell and others about Anselm's 'strongest argument that this (...*either* God is not that than which nothing greater can be thought, *or* is not understood nor thought of...) is false...[being]...to appeal to your faith and to your conscience' (*Reply* I, p. 169) — that it shows Anselm's concern in the *Reply*, and by extension in the *Proslogion* itself, to be with the believer rather than the atheist — ignores this. Anselm is saying to Gaunilo that as a Christian he cannot seriously pretend not to understand 'God'; whereas the Fool can be brought to an understanding of 'that than which nothing greater can be thought' by reference to things which he does understand (see the latter part of *Reply* I). And this is why Anselm refers far more to that than which nothing greater can be thought than to God in his *Reply*; he is concerned to *show to Gaunilo* that his argument *against the Fool* is sound. That argument rests on his definition of God because that is the basis on which he can begin to argue against him, the metaphysics they have in common.[13] Thus there is no question of (mis)interpreting Anselm either fideistically or rationalistically. As Jasper Hopkins rightly points out, '...the very arguments which enlighten believers in their faith likewise help to remove obstacles which keep unbelievers from faith'.[14] An argument which succeeds against the unbeliever cannot but enlighten the believer, otherwise it would not be a sound argument: in contradistinction to neo-Wittgensteinian talk of different language-games, to a greater or lesser extent discrete, Anselm insists on the unity of reason. God, after all, is truth, whether or not the Fool acknowledges this: and the Truth is One.[15] Thus Anselm is able to conduct his argument on the basis that unbelievers 'appeal to reason because they do not believe but we, on the other hand, because we do believe; nevertheless the thing sought is one and the same' (*Cur Deus Homo* I, II, p. 182).

But a fideistic interpretation cannot be dismissed quite so quickly. For in *Proslogion* I Anselm makes this comment on his enterprise:

> For I do not seek to understand so that I may believe; but I believe so that I may understand. For I believe this also, that 'unless I believe, I shall not understand' [Isaiah vii 9]. —p. 115

Surely Anselm is saying here that faith, belief in God, is a prerequisite of understanding his argument. Faith, not reason, must ultimately persuade us that God exists. Is Barth not right to focus on this statement in his determinedly anti-philosophical interpretation of the argument as a theological exposition of the nature of the Christian's belief in God, rather than as any attempt to show the atheist that he is mistaken in his atheism? Faith in God is the edifice on which the argument does, after all, rest: understanding is grounded in faith, for Anselm as for Barth. And yet Anselm expects the Fool — whom he does address, and who does not believe — to understand. Barth's solution is to suggest that the role of the Fool is to confirm that only the believer is in a position properly to understand, since he, the Fool, being a fool, cannot but fail so to understand. (He is not explicit about precisely what it is that the Fool cannot understand, but it seems clear that it is, in the first place, God.) Importantly, however, the world inhabited by the Fool is not a world from which knowledge *per se* is absent. 'The *insipiens*,' Barth writes, 'seems to confront him as living confutation of his proof: he can think of God as not existing. Anselm does not deny this fact...he is an *insipiens* and as such thinks on a level where one can only think falsely — though without violating the inner consistency of that level.'[16] On Barth's view, the Fool can without inconsistency continue to think as he does, on the Fool's own "level". No trans-categorical reasons can be given him for abandoning his thinking for that of the Christian, with its Christian categories. Conversion to Christianity, then, must be entirely a matter of faith, and notional assent to Christian tenets can be given only after the appropriate leap of faith. Reasons can be understood as reasons only within the terms of the Christian's and non-Christian's categories respectively. What counts as a reason for belief for the Christian (e.g., the Word of God as revealed in the Bible) does not count as such for the non-Christian, because for him it is something different (e.g., ancient history and mythology). All the theologian can do is *present* what he takes to be the case; this is why Barth is so averse to natural theology, regarding it as a category mistake of the most drastic kind. The theologian can apparently present the non-believer with something, even though he cannot argue with him.[17] Yet the contradiction with which Anselm maintains the Fool finds himself saddled if he denies that there is a God after having assented to the proposition that God is that than which nothing greater can be thought is *just that*, a contradiction, and certainly not some sort of "contradiction" between "levels" of thought. When explaining, in ch. IV, how it is that the Fool was able to deny that there is a God, Anselm says that it was because he did not understand 'the very object which the thing is' (the thing, that is, to which the word 'God' is applied); he did not understand that the denial of God is a self-contradiction because he did not understand the logical import of the definition of God as that than which nothing greater can be thought. In saying, 'There is no God', the Fool used 'God' without knowing what it meant. Anselm clearly does not think such knowledge impossible in the absence of faith, for he concludes the previous chapter with these words: 'Why then did "the Fool say in his heart, there is no God" [Ps. xiii, I, lii. I] when it is so evident *to any rational mind* that You of all things exist to the highest degree? Why indeed, unless *because he was stupid and a fool*?' (p. 119, my italics) If it is truly the case that it is 'evident to any rational mind' that there is a God, then the Fool, if he continues to deny that there is a God, is irrational: in which case, how can he think 'without violating the inner consistency' of his thinking? Anselm's whole argument is directed towards showing that the Fool is thinking inconsistently, and thus irrationally, if, after having attended to Anselm's argument, he persists in his atheism.

Nevertheless, Anselm has said that he believes that he

should not understand unless he believed; and yet he expects the Fool to understand the argument as it proceeds, although he does not believe. Clearly this stands in need of explanation. Just what is it that Anselm believes that he should not understand but for his belief? It cannot be his own argument, if he believes, as he does, that the Fool is capable of understanding it. These are the two sentences immediately preceding Anselm's avowal: 'I do not try, Lord, to attain Your lofty heights, because my understanding is in no way equal to it. But I do desire to understand Your truth a little, that truth that my heart believes and loves.' (*Pros*. I, p. 115) What Anselm believes he needs to believe in order to understand it, appears to be God's truth, a truth he both believes and loves. It is surely reasonable to suppose that it is the existential import of God's truth that Anselm is considering: it is existential assent, as distinguished from notional assent, that he has in mind here.[18] For a Christian, notional assent, the sort of assent Anselm is seeking to show that even the Fool cannot consistently withold, is inadequate; and the sort of understanding of God necessary for a Christian life is a matter of faith, trust, belief. The understanding necessary for a Christian life is a very different sort of understanding from the purely intellectual understanding of which Anselm believes the Fool to be capable, even though, of course, existential understanding may be attained by the newly-converted Christian after he has attained intellectual understanding. However, such existential understanding is neither necessary for *coming to* a Christian faith, nor sufficient to ensure the fullness of such faith, the fullness which demands complete trust in, and self-subordination to God. But, as Barth agrees,[19] it is necessary for the fullness of faith. (As a monk of course, Anselm would have aimed at precisely such faith.) It is Anselm's whole point that only notional assent and no more is required of the Fool to show that his denial of the existence of God is *inconsistent* — and not, like Peter's denial of Christ for instance, *a betrayal*. The 'fullness' of God's truth is, after all, such as to preclude full understanding of it on anyone's part, including Anselm's:

> For how great [*quanta*] is that light from which shines every truth that gives light to the understanding! How complete is that truth in which is everything that is true and outside of which

> nothing exists save nothingness and falsity! How boundless is that which in one glance sees everything that has been made, and by whom and through whom and in what manner it was made from nothing! What purity, what simplicity, what certitude and splendour is there! Truly it is more than can be understood by any creature. —*Proslogion* XIV, pp. 135—7

> Therefore, Lord, not only are You that than which a greater cannot be thought, but You are also something greater than can be thought... —*Proslogion* XV, p. 137

Anselm certainly acknowledges that his capacity to understand anything at all about God is a gift of God: but that is not to say, as a Barthian position would imply, that such understanding is possible only on the basis of faith. Could my soul, Anselm asks, 'understand anything at all about You save through "Your light and Your truth" [ps. xlii. 3]? If, then, it saw the light and the truth, it saw You. If it did not see You, then it did not see the light or the truth. Or is it that it saw both the truth and the light, and yet it did not see You because it saw You only partially but did not see You as You are?' (*Pros*. XIV, p. 135) It is through God's 'light and truth' that understanding is possible, and for Anselm that is an epistemological fact, true of the understanding of everyone, whether or not he himself believes in God. It is thanks to God that the Fool is able to understand God, as well as anything else he understands, whether or not he himself acknowledges the fact. God, after all, is the creator, the source of being, so that Anselm would agree with Barth when he writes:

> The reason why there is such a thing as existence is that God exists. With his existence stands or falls the existence of all beings that are distinct from him...it is the existence of God that is the criterion of general existence...he and he alone is objective reality. Because God exists in the inexplicable manner which thought cannot dismiss...for that reason there is objective reality and the possibility of its being conceived... —op.cit., pp. 154—5

Where they differ, and differ crucially, is in their epistemology, and not in their ontology: in Barth's case, but not in Anselm's, epistemology is grounded in Christian faith. When Barth writes that 'the knowledge of all other existences (just the opposite of what Gaunilo thinks) stands or falls with the knowledge of this [God's] Existence',²⁰ he implies that knowledge of God, which is possible only for those who believe in God, is a necessary condition of true knowledge of anything at all.²¹ Anselm's position, however, is that certain things about God can be known by anyone. Once the argument is understood by the Fool, and understood to be rationally compelling, then, if the Fool is rational, he must believe that there is a God. It is on that basis that his faith can develop, and that he can come to appreciate more about God than merely knowing that he is real and what certain of his attributes are, which is, after all, only a beginning for the Christian.

When Anselm writes in his Preface to the *Proslogion* that its title was originally to be *Faith in Search of Understanding*, this is to be best understood as referring to his search for 'one single argument that for its proof required no other save itself, and that by itself would suffice to prove that God really exists, that He is the supreme good needing no other and is He whom all things have need of for their being and well-being, and also to prove whatever we believe about the Divine Being' (p. 103), an argument rationally compelling for everyone, one which Anselm felt it incumbent on him, as a Christian, a man of faith, to find. That he wrote it 'from the point of view of one trying to raise his mind to contemplate God and seeking to understand what he believes' (ibid.) in no way implies that it was written only for those sharing that point of view: intellectual argument was a religious duty for Anselm.²² Nowhere in the *Proslogion* is it suggested that any beings have need of *knowledge* of God for their knowledge of being, or of anything else, or that such knowledge must be grounded in faith. Nor is there any mention of faith as a prerequisite of knowledge, either of God or of anything else, in *De Veritate*,²³ where one would expect to find such a claim at least implicitly made, were Barth correct.

Anselm's formula, then, is a definition; and a definition on the basis of which he seeks to convince the atheist of his error. This is why it is couched in terms of 'that than which nothing greater can be thought', rather than 'that which is greatest'. 'Greatest' could be only a description, contingently true of its referent; as a description, even if now true, it could have been, or could in future be, false. This is the gist of Anselm's reason, in *Reply* V, for pointing out to Gaunilo in no uncertain manner that 'nowhere in all that I have said will you find such an argument, [that that which is greater than everything exists in the mind...]' (p. 179):

> For it is not as evident that that which can be thought of as not existing is not that which is greater than everything, as that it is not that than which a greater cannot be thought. And, in the same way, neither is it indubitable that, if there is something which is 'greater than everything', it is identical with 'that than which a greater cannot be thought'; nor, if there were [such a being], that no other like it might exist — as this is certain in respect of what is said to be 'that than which nothing greater can be thought'. For what if someone should say that something that is greater than everything actually exists, and yet that this same being can be thought of as not existing, and that something greater than it can be thought, even if this does not exist? —p. 181

'That than which a greater cannot be thought' cannot refer to something which can be thought not to exist, whereas 'that which is greater than everything' can do so. For given that it is possible that there is something which cannot be thought not to exist, this will be greater, if it exists, than anything that can be thought not to exist — and it could be that the greatest thing there actually happens to be is something which can be thought not to be, in which case it would not be the greatest thing that can be conceived. The referent of 'that which is greater than everything' could be a dependent, temporal entity; but, given that an eternal, self-sufficient entity is conceivable, such an entity could not be the greatest possible entity, since 'whatever can be thought of as not existing...if it does not exist, indeed even if it should exist, (it) would not be that than which a greater cannot be thought' (pp. 179–181). 'That which is greater than everything' is a description *de re*: and as the Fool disagrees with Anselm about what is the case *de re*, no such description can serve as something to which both may accede. It is for the same reason that Anselm does not simply say that God is 'that than which there can be nothing greater'; this is for him a description *de re*, since 'potest esse', as I argued in ch. 2, makes a claim about what we should call a factual state of affairs, rather than about thought, i.e., about what we should call logical possibility. That nothing greater can be thought, since it is the case because there can be nothing greater, is evidence of the latter: and this of course is the basis on which

Anselm seeks to convince the Fool. Consideration of why he chooses just the formula he does, and not some other wording, not only makes clear how Anselm intends his argument to succeed against the Fool, but also serves to confirm that the formula is indeed a definition and not a description.

That than which nothing greater can be thought and that which is greater than everything are in fact one and the same entity. That this is so, however, must wait on a proof that the greatest possible entity exists — in which case it will of course be the greatest entity there is. Only if there indeed exists something which cannot be thought not to exist is there a unique, independent, self-sufficient entity. If there is no such entity, then whatever it is which is the greatest there is might in fact be one of a number of things, depending on the metaphysics involved: all the material objects there are, for example. One can always conceive of something more real than the most real thing there *happens* to be. But, by definition, nothing more real than God can be conceived. Therefore God cannot be the most real thing there happens to be, but rather the most real thing there can be; and this cannot be a description of God, since descriptions can have been, and can come to be, false. 'The most real thing possible' must define, and not describe, God.

Anselm will go on to argue that the most real entity possible cannot be a fiction, otherwise it would not be the most real entity possible. That is why he fastens onto 'greatness' for his formula, and not onto an attribute of God such as his sustaining the world. Such an attribute could be an attribute of a fiction: if the world is sustained, and there is therefore something which sustains it, then whatever that is must be non-fictional. But, of course, there is no reason why the Fool should accept that the world is sustained — or moved, created, designed, etc. Against all these, it may be said that they require the assumption of God's existing for their explication and understanding. What makes this argument different from all versions of the cosmological, however, is that it avoids precisely this problem. Rather, something actually *believed by the unbeliever* is shown to imply that God exists. What is assumed is not some empirical or quasi-empirical belief about the world, but a shared metaphysics.

Nevertheless, Anselm's definition is, on his own admission, incomplete in two ways. It incompletely specifies what God is: and it cannot be fully understood, either by the Fool, or by the believer. It is important to distinguish between the implications of this for an assessment of the validity or otherwise of Anselm's argument, and its implications for the truth of his conclusion. Here I am concerned only with the former.

In ch. XV of the *Proslogion*, as we saw earlier, Anselm writes that

> You are also something greater than can be thought. For since it is possible to think that there is such a one, then, if You are not this same being, something greater than You could be thought — which cannot be. —p. 137

God is more real than we can conceive: the formula, therefore, cannot tell us exactly what he is like. Rather it gives us the conditions which it is necessary for x to meet if x is God, but not the sufficient conditions. It is a partial definition, rather as 'a spherical object' is a partial definition of a football. If x is a football, then x must be spherical; but that x is spherical is not sufficient for it to be a football. Nevertheless, logical features about the definiendum may be deduced from partial definitions. Indeed, that is their use: '..."that than which a greater cannot be thought" is understood and is in the mind to the extent that we understand these things [that it exists as a whole, etc.] about it' (*Reply* I, p. 173). Whether or not sufficient can be deduced from Anselm's partial definition to enable us to know what we are talking about when we talk about God, is of course the crucial question about Anselm's conclusion (see ch. 5). Nor can even this admittedly partial definition be fully understood by the Fool, who can merely 'form an idea from other things of "that than which a greater cannot be thought"' (*Reply* VIII, p. 187), and understands it 'in some way' (*Reply* VII, p. 185). In fact, Anselm is committed to the view that neither the Fool nor the believer can *fully* understand the formula — although he nowhere states this explicitly — because of what he says in *Pros.* XV. If God is more real than can be conceived, and if a partial definition of God is that he is that entity which is the most real possible, then, to the extent that God's reality cannot be conceived, to that extent the partial definition of him likewise cannot be conceived.

The question of the intelligibility of Anselm's formula must of course be central in any critique of the argument: is it the case that that than which a greater cannot be thought can be conceived to exist in reality (step 5)? Gaunilo writes:

> ...I can so little think of or entertain in my mind this being (that which is greater than all those others that are able to be thought of, and which is said to be none other than God Himself) in terms of an object known to me either by species or genus, as I can think of God Himself, whom indeed for this very reason I can even think does not exist. For neither do I know the reality itself, nor can I form an idea from some other things like it since, as you say yourself, it is such that nothing could be like it.
> —*Reply on Behalf of the Fool*, 4, p. 161

Gaunilo's point here is in fact, if perhaps not by intention, directed against the entire metaphysical framework within which the argument takes place. It is remarkable that this passage, foreshadowing as it does Aquinas's later objections, has been ignored — entirely ignored as far as I know — in contemporary discussions of Anselm's argument. If whatever it is which is such that nothing greater can be thought is quite different from anything else, then how can I know what it is like? The point is of course one which has often been made against the intelligibility of Plato's Forms. Further, and this is where the similarity to Aquinas is most noticeable, if God is defined as that than which nothing greater can be thought, then, if the definition is unknowable, God himself cannot be known. Anselm's reply to this is very interesting:

> For since everything that is less good is similar in so far as it is good to that which is more good, it is evident to every rational mind that, mounting from the less good to the more good we can from those things than which something greater can be thought conjecture a great deal about that than which a greater cannot be thought. Who, for example, cannot think of this (even if he does not believe that what he thinks of actually exists) namely, that if something that has a beginning and end is good, that which, although it has had a beginning, does not, however, have an end, is much better? And just as this latter is better than the former, so also that which has neither beginning nor end is better again than this, even if it passes always from the past through the present to the future. Again, whether something of this kind actually exists or not, that which does not lack anything at all, nor is forced to change or move, is very much better still. Cannot this be thought? Or can we think of something greater than this? Or is not this precisely to form an idea of that than which a greater cannot be thought from those things than which a greater

can be thought? There is, then, a way by which one can form an idea of 'that than which a greater cannot be thought'.
—*Reply* VIII, p. 187

It is not clear whether he intends to suggest that one may obtain an idea of that than which nothing greater can be thought by intellectually ascending from good to better entities; or by ascending from inferior to greater entities in the same sort of way in which one might ascend from good to better entities. The former seems the more likely, in which case his deduction of value from ontological status in chs. V ff. of the *Proslogion* may have led him not to distinguish between the two in his *Reply* to Gaunilo. Perhaps it is his eagerness to show that he is not presupposing the existence of that than which nothing greater can be thought that induces him to conflate the two: for 'that which does not lack anything at all, nor is forced to change or move' may be better than something which does lack certain things, etc. whether or not it (the former) actually exists, but it certainly cannot be greater, more real, unless it does exist. On the other hand, 'something of this kind' may refer forward and not back — in which case see p. 59 ff. What is clear is that Anselm is suggesting that a conception of that than which nothing greater can be thought may be built up by means of a *via negativa*. The entity in question cannot be temporal, nor dependent for its existence on anything else: thus it must be eternal and self-sufficient. Gaunilo is wrong in thinking that no idea whatsoever can be formed of that than which nothing greater can be thought. Nevertheless, as I shall go on to argue, whether such an idea as *can* be formed is sufficiently determinate to provide Anselm with a positive conclusion and not merely a valid argument is a problem he does not address: quite naturally, given his platonic assumptions.

Aquinas's basic objection to Anselm's argument also concerns the definition he employs, and its relation to the possibility of knowledge of God. The distinction between something's being self-evident in itself, and its being self-evident to us, which is what is often identified as Aquinas's rebuttal of Anselm, is, as Matthew Cosgrove argues in his definitive paper, 'Thomas Aquinas on Anselm's Argument',[24] an objection to Anselm's conclusion that the Fool cannot deny God's existence without contradiction, rather than an effective reply to Anselm's argument; although it is the basis of what Cosgrove and Gareth Matthews[25] both take to be a conclusive objection. Let me try to make this clear. 'But, since we do not know concerning God what he is,' Aquinas writes, '[the proposition, "God exists"] is not self-evident to us; but needs to be demonstrated through those things which are better known to us and less known according to nature, namely through [his] effects.'[26] But, whether or not Aquinas's distinction between two alleged modes of self-evidence is satisfactory, this is no argument against Anselm, just as Gaunilo's assertion that God is unknowable fails to tell: for it is precisely by defining God as he does that Anselm seeks to show what is known — to the Fool as well as to the believer — about God. The definition of God, which Aquinas himself appears to accept in the *Summa Theologica* (Ia, q.2, a.1, ad.2) does tell us *something* about what he is. Aquinas's objection is no advance on Gaunilo's, although, of course, it raises the same ultimate question as to the nature and extent of what the definition tells us. In fact, Anselm's definition tells us more than Aquinas's claim that the essence of God is to be; and of course Aquinas's own claim that 'we do not know concerning God what he is' raises, even more acutely than Anselm's concessions, the question of our being able to say anything intelligible about God at all.

The argument which Cosgrove picks out, and rightly I believe, as the most important of those Aquinas advances against Anselm is that in *Summa Contra Gentiles* I, 11: 'For it is not a difficulty that given anything either in reality or in the intellect something greater can be thought, save only for him who concedes that there exists something in reality than which a greater cannot be thought.'[27] (I shall not puzzle about the sense of the qualification: if 'something greater can be thought', then surely nobody can make such a concession.) Again, I think Cosgrove is right in rejecting Hartshorne's view of this passage as an espousal of positivism,[28] since 'It is not the impossibility of God existing, but the impossibility of conceiving something so great that a greater cannot conceived, which Thomas thinks a plausible position.'[29] This is of course consistent with his insistence that we do not know what God is, only that he is: we cannot know of God that he is that than which nothing greater can be thought, because that definition is incoherent. Now this is clearly a far more serious objection to the argument than that in the *Summa Theologica*. But would Anselm disagree with Aquinas about the impossibility of conceiving God's greatness? The passage from *Proslogion* XV clearly shows that he would not: 'You are also something greater than can be thought'. Since Anselm appears to hold that eternity and self-sufficiency, plus all the attributes he infers from these, are merely necessary, and not necessary and sufficient, conditions of an entity's being that than which nothing greater can be thought, let us grant that he would agree with Aquinas that 'given anything...a greater can always be thought'. This view relies on the position that the nature of maximal reality cannot be fully determined by thought, at least not by our thought, a position which Anselm and Aquinas share precisely because they hold that that entity which they take to be the most real entity there is, namely God, is not fully knowable (in Anselm's case) or not knowable at all (in Aquinas's case). The contradiction that there might appear to be between ch.XV and ch.II evaporates as soon as we remember that 'You are that than which nothing greater can be thought' is a partial definition, one which is not fully determinative of its subject. Ch. XV describes what is defined in ch. II; the description is deducible from the definition.

The point is that if we take 'that than which nothing greater can be thought' as Aquinas appears to have done, and as Matthews and Cosgrove do, namely as referring to a definite, specifiable entity, then Aquinas's criticism is in order. It is indeed impossible to conceive something so great that a greater cannot be conceived. But this is crucially ambiguous. Does it mean that it is impossible to conceive a specific entity which is unsurpassably great, or that it is impossible to conceive that there is an unsurpassably great entity? In the context of Aquinas, it clearly means the former: '*given* [my italics] anything either in reality or in the intellect, something greater can be thought...'.[30] Matthews' comment on this passage[31] relies on taking the phrase like this, and he is right in thinking that, however great any entity one cares to name may be, it is always in principle possible to conceive a greater (given that the nature of maximal reality cannot be fully determined). Anselm, however, did not mean

55

by 'God is that than which nothing greater can be thought' that God is a definite, specifiable entity; rather, God is *whatever* is such that nothing greater can be conceived. Anselm does not need to hold that we are able to conceive what that specific entity is like, which is so great that nothing greater can be thought, nor even that we can conceive exactly what God's greatness itself is like. He maintains only that the degree of God's greatness is the highest possible degree. Matthews himself notices precisely this point: 'Prima facie, it is a special virtue of Anselm's ontological argument, as contrasted with, say, Descartes's that it would seem to hold even though we do not have a "clear and distinct idea" of God. All we need to know is that God is something a greater than which cannot be conceived.'[32] If this is the case, however, then his analysis, while correctly interpreting Aquinas, fails to strike against Anselm. He writes:

> Instead he [the atheist] can say this:
>
> 2) For any given thing, a greater thing can always be conceived.
>
> (2) is the logical equivalent of this:
>
> 3) There is nothing than which a greater cannot be conceived.
>
> (2) and (3) are the contradictory of this:
>
> 4') There is something than which a greater cannot be conceived.[33]

But (2) is the logical equivalent of (3) only if (3) is taken to mean that there is no entity which we can exhaustively specify and of which we can truly say that no greater entity than this is conceivable. However, (3) may be taken as meaning that we cannot conceive of there being anything such that nothing greater than it is possible: and only if it is thus taken does it contradict the sense in which Anselm would assert(4'). But in that case it is not the logical equivalent of (2); and nor, of course, would Anselm assent to it. Nor could Aquinas disagree with him, since he also believes that we are able to know that God exists. The point is a familiar one: we can conceive that there is such a thing as God, without being able to specify exactly what that thing is like. This is the crucial distinction which Aquinas appears to fail to apply when criticising Anselm's argument. It is true to say of God, Anselm argues, that it is inconceivable that there should be anything greater than he is, and, *a fortiori*, that nothing greater than he is can be conceived; but that is not to say that God, or his greatness (or, indeed, any other of his attributes) is itself conceivable. If we are unable to conceive anything greater than God, even though God is greater than we can conceive — and there is no contradiction in this — then Aquinas's objection to Anselm's definition has no force. In fact Anselm himself provides the counter-argument in a rather different form, in the course of his reply to Gaunilo's original objection:

> But even if it were true that [the object] that than which a greater cannot be thought cannot be thought of nor understood, it would not, however, be false that [the formula] 'that than which a greater cannot be thought' could be thought of and understood. For just as nothing prevents one from saying 'ineffable' although one cannot specify what is said to be ineffable; and just as one can think of the inconceivable — although one cannot think of what 'inconceivable' applies to — so also, when 'that than which a greater cannot be thought' is spoken of, there is no doubt at all that what is heard can be thought of and understood even if the thing itself cannot be thought of and understood.
> — *Reply* IX, pp. 187—9

Having dealt with steps (1) and (5) of the argument, I shall now consider Anselm's comparison of what is 'in reality' with what is 'in the mind' ((2), (3), and (6)).

In *Reply* II, Anselm writes:

> Observe, then, that from the fact that it is understood, it does follow that it is in the mind. For, just as what is thought is thought by means of a thought, and what is thought by a thought is thus, as thought, *in* thought, so also, what is understood is understood by the mind, and what is understood by the mind is thus, as understood, *in* the mind. What could be more obvious than this?
> —pp. 173—4

If I think of Canterbury Cathedral, it is in my thought; if I understand the phrase, 'the tallest man in Canterbury', then it is in my mind. Although we should not care to put it like this, it is clear that for Anselm 'to be understood' is synonymous with 'to be in the mind'. But this is ambiguous. What is understood is the definite description, 'the tallest man in

Canterbury'; but what is in the mind is the tallest man in Canterbury. Otherwise, (6) would compare entities with propositions. Whereas what is thought of may perhaps be said to be in the mind ('Whom did you have in mind?') and this is simply another way of saying that it is thought of, what is understood is not the same as what one has in mind or what might be said to be in the mind. (Unless we are talking of understanding people: 'I just can't understand old Fred.' Maybe I do have old Fred in mind when I say this.) Expressions are understood; and if anything is in the mind in any sense at all, it is their referents. To talk in this context of 'that than which nothing greater can be thought' as being in the mind, therefore, is misleading, since it is *not* the same as saying that it is understood. What Anselm means, of course, is that if the phrase 'that than which nothing greater can be thought' is understood, then it is obviously intelligible, or conceivable; it makes sense. And if it makes sense, then it has a possible referent; its referent may exist. While it is true that 'x is in the mind' differs from 'x is logically possible' in that it suggests a reference to a person, whereas the latter phrase does not, this is misconceived as an objection to Charlesworth's interpretation of 'est in intellectu' as 'is logically possible'.[34] There are doubtless some logically possible entities which have not as yet been conceived by anyone; but precisely because logically possible, they are conceivable. If x has been conceived by someone, then, trivially, x can be conceived, or is conceivable. And to say that x is conceivable is to say that x is logically possible. 'X is logically possible' cannot be taken as 'x is in such-and-such's mind': but 'x is in such-and-such's mind', while it may not mean 'x is logically possible', certainly implies that it is. Even if (3) does not mean 'it [the formula] is logically possible', it implies exactly that. The following amendments may therefore be made to the argument:

(3.1) it is therefore logically possible.
(4.1) Assume that that than which nothing greater can be thought does not exist in reality, but is merely logically possible.
(6.1) To exist in reality is greater than to be merely logically possible.
(9.1) Therefore there is absolutely no doubt that something than which nothing greater can be thought exists in reality, and is not merely logically possible.

How is (6.1) to be understood? To exist in reality, Anselm says, is *greater*, ontologically greater, than to be merely logically possible. The paradox of an actual evil being 'better' than a possible one is thus ruled out at the start. Nor need we worry about the difficulties involved in trying to compare £1000 with a possible £1000, which 'is not some queer ghost-like kind of (actual, real) money...not a sum of money, albeit of a peculiar kind',[35] by saying that £1000 has all the properties of a possible £1000, plus existence. This is not because 'exists' is a unique kind of predicate (although it may be), or because God's uniqueness allows predicates attaching to him to escape the usual logical demands made of them (although they may do). Rather it is because, as Charlesworth suggests, 'A conceptual £100 is greater than a conceptual £50 [in a quantitative, non-Anselmian sense of 'greater'] and a real £100 is greater than a real £50; but in Anselm's sense a real £50 is "greater" than a conceptual £100.'[36] To put it another way, Anselm compares actual existence with logical possibility. The ontological scale which is used to make such comparisons compares classes, and not individuals. Anything which belongs to the class of those things which exist (non-fictions) is greater than anything which belongs to the class of those things which are merely logically possible (fictions). It is important to see that this is Anselm's procedure and that he is not simply comparing a fictional with a non-fictional God: that is, (6.1) above refers not to single entities, but to two sorts of things, fictions and non-fictions.

Anselm's principle as stated in *Proslogion* II appears to have misled commentators: 'For if it exists solely in the mind even, it can be thought to exist in reality also, which is greater.' This may give the impression, especially if it is assumed that Anselm is talking in terms of perfection and arguing that existence is an attribute making for it, that a fictional God is being compared with a non-fictional God. The passage from *Reply* VIII quoted earlier (pp. 52–3) may suggest such a view even more strongly: 'Again, whether something of this kind actually exists or not, that which does not lack anything at all, nor is forced to change or move, is very much better [= greater?] still.' (p. 187) Unless Anselm is simply making a mistake here, and forgetting that actually existing is a necessary condition of something's being greater than any given existent, it would appear that he is thinking of existence as an attribute, with the result that the scale of reality with which he is working is not that described in ch. 2, but rather something like this:

> Most real possible non-fiction
> Most real possible fiction
>
> Non-fictional physical object
> Fictional physical object

Indeed, just such a view is attributed to Anselm by Paul Miller, who supposes Anselm to be arguing that 'That which lacks nothing which would make it the greatest conceivable being must necessarily exist, since existence is a thinkable perfection adding to the greatness of that to which it is predicated.'[37] But such a scale of reality is clearly absurd: why should, for instance, a fictional star be more real than a non-fictional earthworm (given for the sake of argument that stars, being everlasting, as Anselm takes them to be, are higher up the scale than earthworms)? For as we have seen, it is the degree of ontological independence of an entity which determines its relative position on the platonic scale; and all fictions are less ontologically independent than any non-fiction. Admittedly neither Plato nor Anselm put the matter in these terms. Nevertheless, if this were not an accurate interpretation of the scale, then I do not see how Anselm's principle could be used to show that God exists in reality (is non-fictional). For if the principle were limited in application to God, and thus applied to nothing else at all, what grounds would there be for supposing it to hold? And if it were limited in application to fictional and non-fictional examples of individual entities, what grounds would there be for supposing a non-fictional x to be greater than a fictional y? If its being a fiction made a fictional tree less real than a non-fictional tree, then how could a fictional angel be more real than a non-fictional tree? 'Real' would be used in two quite different ways, with the result that the whole notion of a scale would collapse, and we would be left able to make comparisons in respect of reality only of fictional with non-fictional individuals. This would go against all the evidence of Anselm's writings as discussed in ch. 2. I think it a not unreasonable supposition, therefore, that if the passage in *Reply* VIII is to be interpreted in this way, then it is just a mistake on Anselm's part. On the other hand, that this would appear to be the case might well suggest that 'something of this kind' (p. 52) should be taken as referring back, and not forward.

I suspect it is his neglecting that Anselm's principle asserts that any non-fiction is more real than any fiction which lies also behind D. P. Henry's curious counter-argument against the conclusion of *Proslogion* II in *Medieval Logic and Metaphysics*.[38] Since it might appear initially plausible, and would certainly dispose of Anselm's argument without further ado were that plausibility to be confirmed, I shall discuss it in some detail. Henry writes:

> Hence on his own principles the vital section of the argument which we have been considering could equally well (or even more feasibly) read:
> 3.20 It is certain that that-than-which-a-more-great-cannot-be-thought must only be in the understanding.
> 3.21 For if it is at least in the understanding, it cannot be thought also to exist in fact, since this would be more great.
> 3.22 On this account if that-than-which-a-more-great-cannot-be-thought exists in fact, then
> 3.221 that very thing than which a more great is *not* able to be thought is that than which a more great *is* able to be thought.
> 3.3 But obviously this (3.221) cannot be.
> 3.4 Hence without any doubt something-than-which-a-more-great-is-not-able-to-be-thought cannot exist both in the understanding and in fact.
> -ibid., p. 117

One way of seeing what is wrong with this is to recall that Anselm's principle is that anything in reality is greater than anything in the understanding alone. Thus, nothing which is in the understanding alone can be that than which nothing greater can be thought, since given that there is something in reality, the latter is (or are all) greater than anything in the understanding alone. (3.221) is therefore not the contradiction produced. Rather, this contradiction arises:

> 3.221' that very thing than which a more great is *not* able to be thought is that than which everything in reality is greater.

And the conclusion must therefore be modified as follows:

3.4' Hence without any doubt something which does not exist in reality cannot be that-than-which-a-more-great-is-not-able-to-be-thought.

What this shows is that the alternative to Anselm's claim that that than which nothing greater can be thought is a non-fiction (exists in reality and in the understanding) is that it is nonsense, existing therefore neither in reality, nor in the understanding — since it cannot be thought at all. But this I shall examine later.

The point to be made here is that if God were merely a logical possibility then anything existent — a statue of Apollo, the person next door, this sheet of paper — would be greater than he; but, since he is that than which *nothing* greater can be thought, this cannot be the case. God is not the god than which a greater god cannot be thought, but that thing than which nothing greater can be thought. He is ontologically superior to anything and everything else. The ontological class of which he is the sole member is superior to all other ontological classes, which are comprised by everything else there is. Now, if x is logically possible, but does not exist, or has never existed, then x is a figment of the imagination, a mythical entity, a fictional entity, or some other product of the human mind. If x is not a fiction, although logically possible, if, that is, it is a logically possible entity which has not yet been conceived by anyone — allowing that we can intelligibly talk of such an entity at all — then it either exists, or has existed but no longer exists. And if x is logically possible ('est in intellectu') and exists ('est in re'), or has existed, then it cannot of course be a fiction. This is the force of Anselm's comparison in (6): existents are greater than fictions. I shall therefore make some further amendments to my statement of the argument:

(4.2) Assume that that than which nothing greater can be thought is an entity which does not exist, but is a fiction.

(6.2) Any entity which exists is greater than any entity which is a fiction.

(9.2) Therefore there is absolutely no doubt that that than which nothing greater can be thought is an existent entity, and not a fiction.

In order to become clearer about (6.2), and to see just how

it shows that criticisms in terms of the dogma that existence is not a predicate are irrelevant, it will be helpful to examine in some detail elements of Plantinga's acute discussion in *God and Other Minds*.[39] Having discussed the question of existence and predication, he concludes with the following restatement of the argument:

> Finally, Anselm's argument can easily be restated so that the notion of existence in the understanding plays no part in it, in which case it cannot be thought to involve predicating real existence of a being presupposed to exist in the understanding:
> (1) Suppose that the being than which it is not possible that there be a greater does not exist (assumption for reductio).
> (2) Any existent being is greater than any non-existent being.
> (3) The Taj Mahal exists.
> (4) Hence the Taj Mahal is greater than the being than which it is not possible that there be a greater (1,2,3).
>
> (4) is necessarily false; hence the assumption of (1), (2) and (3) is necessarily false. (2) is necessarily true. Therefore, the conjunction of (1) and (3) is necessarily false; and so 'The Taj Mahal exists' entails 'The being than which none greater can be conceived exists'. But the former proposition is obviously true; hence the latter is, too. —ibid., pp. 62–3

The following chapter centres around (2), several possible interpretations of which Plantinga uses to generate unacceptable conclusions from arguments of the same form as his restatement of Anselm's. In attempting to explicate (2), he tries various formulations in terms of A and B sharing the same properties and having no other properties besides those shared, the sole difference between them being that A exists and B does not — and this makes A greater than B. Plantinga rejects all of these formulations,[40] as of course he must if he is to make sense of Anselm's principle. For if A exists and B does not, then whatever properties either may have or lack, A is greater than B; their properties have no bearing on their ontological greatness. Indeed, Plantinga arrives at a formulation of (2) which shows just that:

(2e) If A exists and B does not, then A is greater than B.[41]

The first unacceptable conclusion he generates is that 'obviously in this way we can go on to prove the existence of the greatest possible thing of any kind you please',[42] using as his example 'The greatest possible horse', which 'is to be read as "the horse than which it is not possible that there be a greater"'.⁴³ But, as was shown in the discussion of Gaunilo's 'perfect island', this is nonsense. No horse can be ontologically greater than any other horse. The second conclusion is that 'by using this form of argument we can show that God both does and does not exist'.⁴⁴ But the premiss '(1) The being greater than a does not exist' (where 'a' is 'a greatest actual being')⁴⁵ is nonsensical, unless it is taken to mean that there is no being greater than a, which is clearly not what Plantinga intends, for his argument runs:

> (2e) If A exists and B does not, then A is greater than B.
> (3) The Taj Mahal exists.
> .
> .
> .
> (6) The Taj Mahal is greater than the being greater than a — (2e), (3).⁴⁶

(6) suggests that there is some being greater than a, some fictional being greater than the greatest actual being: but no fictional being can be greater than the greatest actual being, or greater than any actual being for that matter. The suggestion in (1), that there is a being greater than a, but that that being is not an existent, is nonsense. If (1) were taken to mean that there is no being greater than a, then it would of course be trivially true — if a is the greatest actual being, then there cannot be any being greater than it, since actuality (= reality) is the measure of greatness. The concept, 'the being greater than a' is self-contradictory. The same line of reasoning may be applied to Plantinga's next argument, in which he concludes that by (2e), 'if there are any Guatemalans at all, there is an infinite set of them'.⁴⁷ The argument relies on the following:

> ...Suppose there is at least one [Guatemalan], and call him Hector. Now there is a Guatemalan greater than Hector. For suppose there is none: then the Guatemalan greater than Hector does not exist. But then by (2e) Hector is greater than the Guatemalan greater than Hector.⁴⁸

The notion of a Guatemalan greater than Hector is, if Hector exists, nonsense; the idea to which such a supposition gives rise, that 'the Guatemalan greater than Hector does not exist', is fallacious in suggesting that there is such a Guatemalan, but that he is a non-existent Guatemalan. There simply is no Guatemalan greater than Hector, given that Hector is an existent Guatemalan. The supposition that there is none does not lead to the conclusion that there is a non-existent one.

Plantinga's misunderstanding of the concept of greatness is clearly revealed when he considers

> (6″) The greatest possible being does not exist and the greatest possible being is (for that very reason) a lesser being than the Taj Mahal.[49]

He says that (6″) 'does not at any rate *appear* to be necessarily false'.[50] But of course it makes no sense. If any existent being is greater than any non-existent being (Plantinga's (2e), my (6.2)), then the greatest possible being cannot be a non-existent being. And that is precisely Anselm's conclusion (9.2): Therefore there is absolutely no doubt that that than which nothing greater can be thought is an existent entity, and not a fiction.

To return to (6.2): in discussing Plantinga, I argued that the notion of a non-existent being, a fiction, which is greater than an existent being is nonsense. Now if that is the case, then (6.2) is a necessary proposition. If it is true that 'the merest earthworm really [is] a good deal more impressive than the most exalted but merely fictitious being',[51] then it is contingently true. An earthworm *need not* be more impressive than any fictitious entity: Lady Macbeth, for instance, may be a good deal more impressive than any earthworm. But she cannot be greater: for existence is a necessary condition of greatness. If (6.2) were taken as a contingent statement, then what grounds would there be for supposing it to be true? If it is not logically impossible that any existent entity should be greater than any fiction, then 'greater' must be understood in the same sort of way as 'more impressive' was understood above, that is, as a description over the correct application of which there can be disagreement, without there being disagreement about the facts of the matter. People might admit that an earthworm is a living organism and Lady Macbeth the product of Shakespeare's imagination, but yet disagree as to which is the more impressive. If I agree that Jones measures 6ft., and Brown 5ft. 10ins., however, it would be irrational not to agree that Jones is taller than Brown; 6ft. is more than 5ft. 10ins., and 'being taller' means 'measuring more'. To take (6.2) as a contingent statement, likening 'greater' to 'more impressive' rather than to 'taller', would demand an answer to the question, What does 'greater' mean? If the answer given were in terms of impressiveness, or any other non-ontological concept, then it would remain to be shown conclusively that existent entities were indeed greater than fictions. I do not see how that could be done. If the answer given were in terms of an ontological concept, on the other hand, then that would show that (6.2) was not a contingent proposition, but a necessary one. And this is indeed the case, because for Anselm greatness entails existence in reality.

If it is necessarily true that any entity which exists is greater than any entity which is a mere fiction, then it follows that it is necessarily true that that than which nothing greater can be thought is an existent entity, and not a fiction: if greatness entails existence in reality, then the greatest possible entity must exist in reality. In its platonic setting, then, Anselm's argument is valid. Clearly it is self-contradictory to maintain of one and the same entity that it is both the most real entity possible, and that it is not real, or does not exist. Anselm succeeds in showing that those who, like the Fool, admit the notion of 'that than which nothing greater can be thought', are thereby committed to the supposition that it actually exists, since this is just what the definition of the entity entails. Those who hold that God does not exist, Anselm might have said — but does not say — cannot hold also that there is anything which is such that nothing greater can be thought. What is more, they must hold that there *cannot* be such an entity, that the notion is nonsense; since, if they thought that it just happened to be the case that there was no such entity, they would be misunderstanding the notion altogether. If the definition is coherent, then whatever particular entity the Fool rejects as a candidate for the object of the definition, some other entity must fit it; for if no entity fitted it, the definition would not define anything. There is no question of including 'the predicate actuality or existence, either openly stated or wrapped up for decency's sake in some other predicate...',[52] in a conception 'hatched in your own *sinciput*',[53] as

Schopenhauer, Kant, et al. have diagnosed as the fundamental sleight of hand involved in the ontological argument. Rather, our attention must be directed to the coherence or otherwise of the metaphysical system on which the argument relies, and of which it is in fact a basic prop; in particular to the coherence or otherwise of Anselm's formula itself. This is precisely what Leibniz saw when he said that 'The Scholastics, not excepting even their Doctor Angelicus, have misunderstood this argument, and have taken it as a paralogism... It is not a paralogism, but it is an imperfect demonstration, which assumes something that must still be proved in order to render it mathematically evident; that is, it is tacitly assumed that this idea of the all-great or all-perfect being is possible, and implies no contradiction.'[54]

The argument is formally valid. Nevertheless, all the crucial questions remain, and may be summed up in asking how 'existence' is related to the 'reality' of the platonic system in which Anselm's argument operates. As with Plato's Forms, so with Anselm's God: he may be defined within a particular metaphysics as supremely real, but does he actually exist?

Before going on to pursue this, however, it is necessary to examine in rather closer detail Anselm's debt to Plato, in order to avoid any suggestion that I am claiming that Anselm was, explicitly, a neo-platonist in the Plotinian mould. The argument is platonic, not because it relies on the content of Plato's Theory of Forms, but because it relies on that theory's form. God and the Good occupy similar positions at the summit of a hierarchical system the nature of which they — respectively — determine. The point is that the Judaeo-Christian God must have something in common with the rest of the hierarchy, his creation, in order to be the *most real* entity possible.[55] Precisely this is the crucial merit of Anselm's argument, that it reflects in its structure this central claim, derived as it is from Christianity's Greek inheritance; therein, in fact, lies both its chief significance and the source of its peculiar fascination, as I shall go on to argue. Plato's notion of reality *per se*, however, is not necessary for Anselm's argument: any notion of reality will serve so long as it readily admits of degrees thereof. That is the sense in which it is a platonic argument.[56] Thus it may be stated in a variety of terms — for example, although doubtless without his approval, in Geachian language. Geach writes:

But in fact the proposition 'A God exists' does not ascribe the attribute of existing to some God or other — thus, either to the true God or to some false God — but rather affirms that something-or-other has Divine attributes.[57]

For Anselm's definition of God, then, we may substitute
   (1) The divine attributes are the set of attributes constituting maximal reality (call the set M).
The argument then proceeds as follows:
   (2) Suppose there is nothing which has M; then
   (3) there is nothing which is maximally real.
   (4) But something-or-other must be that which is maximally real (=Anselm's assumption that 'that than which nothing greater can be thought' is coherent).
   (5) Therefore something-or-other has M.
   (6) Since, if x is maximally real, x is real,
   (7) whatever it is which has M is real.
Only if M is a fiction, so that whatever it is which has M — insofar as it has only M — is a fiction, will the argument fail: for it is a necessary condition of M's not being a fiction that 'M' be coherent, i.e., that M is a set of attributes which it is possible for something-or-other to have. The content of M, however, will be determined by the religious and/or metaphysical system within which the argument is located; that is, by the sort of god whose existence is at issue. In the case of the Christian God, as I go on to argue, the attributes concerned — and this is Christianity's directly platonic inheritance — are aseity and atemporality.

The existence of a god with a different metaphysical pedigree would have to be argued for on the basis of different attributes; but the *form* of the argument would remain the same if the relationship of such a god to the world were similarly hierarchical. The existence of a somewhat Hegelian god, for example, might be argued for roughly as follows:
   (1) We believe that our god is the Absolute.
   (2) 'The Absolute' is coherent.
   (3) Suppose the Absolute is a fiction;
   (4) but there is something which is not a fiction.
   (5) Any entity which is not a fiction is more absolute than any entity which is a fiction.
   (6) Therefore (3,4,5) something is more absolute than the Absolute.

(7) 'But this is obviously impossible.'
(8) Therefore there is absolutely no doubt that the Absolute is not a fiction.

As with Anselm's argument, it is the premisses which are problematic. To the extent that such a parallel argument may appropriately be given for the existence of a particular god, to that extent such a god has a platonic pedigree; his relationship to the world is hierarchical. Where no difference of *degree* between a god and the world is postulated, no *ontological* comparison is possible, and so no parallel argument is possible. Where the god concerned does not have a relation to the world similar to that of the God of Christianity, as perhaps in the case of a somewhat Spinozistic god, he is a different sort of god, and his existence a different sort of existence. If, for instance, a god is said to be all there is, then the question of existence does not even arise. Attention is properly focussed on the point of such a definition at all — it becomes interesting only if all there is is not just all there seems to be.

Anselm's argument, then, is platonic inasmuch as the God of Christianity is platonic. And as with the Good, the immediate question must concern the relationship of his reality to that of the world. In the following chapter, therefore, I shall consider some general points about ascriptions of existence, and in particular ascriptions of existence to God; and in ch. 5 discuss in detail the implications of Anselm's argument and its formal validity for an understanding of statements asserting God's existence.

Chapter 4

'Existence' and God

When we say of something that it exists, we often mean to assert that it is ontologically independent of human beings, that it is not something which has been made up. Thus coelacanths and condors *exist*: unlike unicorns or Hamlet, they are not figments of our imagination or creations of our intellect. In brief, the latter are fictions, the former are not. The former are in no way dependent on there being human beings for their being what they are. Coelacanths and condors would in a clear — although not unproblematic sense — *be* a variety of fish and a variety of bird respectively even if there had never been any human beings to conceive of them or to describe them, and would continue to be what they are even after the demise of the human race. That there are such things as coelacanths, condors, etc., is not logically dependent on human thought or imagination. That there are such things as unicorns, however (a variety of mythical beast) and Hamlet (a dramatic character) is logically dependent on human thought or imagination, since there would be no such things as mythical beasts, dramatic characters, etc., if there were no human beings to imagine or conceive them.

An immediate problem is that, whereas the membership of the class of fictions is in principle easy to determine — anything which is, so to speak, entirely a product of some human mental operation is a fiction — the membership of the class of non-fictions is a matter of controversy.

It is tempting to argue, for example, that 'x exists' properly means 'x occupies spatio-temporal position'; and this is doubtless just what it very often does mean. Assuming, reasonably, that material objects exist in space and time, then in those cases where x is some material object, 'x exists', inasmuch as it asserts that there is such a thing as x, that x is not a fiction, asserts that x is in space and time. But this is not the case where x is not a material object. The temptation to insist that 'x exists' is always to be understood as 'x occupies some spatio-temporal position' is a product of the assumption that *only* material objects are non-fictions, that for any x whatever, either x is a material object, or x is a fiction. But of course, this is the case only if the materialists are right, only if it is held that 'x exists' (= 'x occupies some spatio-temporal position') and 'x is a fiction' are the only possible alternatives, so that there can be no non-fictional x which does not exist, but which rather subsists, is, is real, has being, or whatever.

This latter position however, which may be characterized as the thesis that everything is, but not everything exists, is quite unhelpful, since it cannot solve the problem posed by the materialist, namely that of specifying *what* something is, if it neither exists nor is a fiction. Quine characterizes this very conveniently:

> A curious thing about the ontological problem is its simplicity. It can be put in three Anglo-Saxon monosyllables: 'What is there?' It can be answered, moreover, in a word — 'Everything' — and everyone will accept this answer as true. However, this is merely to say that there is what there is. There remains room for disagreement over cases...[1]

The proponent of such a view 'genially grants us the non-existence of Pegasus and then, contrary to what *we* meant by non-existence of Pegasus, insists that Pegasus *is*. Existence is one thing, he says, and subsistence another.'[2] This is what Russell suggested in *Principia Mathematica* when arguing that being is a general attribute of everything, a view which he thought (before formulating his later and better-known position) would solve the problem of negative existentials:

> Being is what belongs to every conceivable term, to every possible object of thought... 'A is not' implies that there is a term, A, whose being is denied, and hence that A is...Numbers, Homeric gods, relations, chimeras, and four-dimensional spaces all have being, for if they were not, we could make no propositions about

them. Thus being is a general attribute of everything, and to mention anything is to show that it is. *Existence*, on the contrary, is the prerogative of some only among beings.[3]

Whatever the merits of this as a solution to the problem of negative existentials, or rather that of reference to non-existents generally, it does not help with the question of the meaning of 'exists' as posed by the materialist, since the solution suggested (that there *are* things which do not exist, yet which are not fictions) is an empty one. If being is a general attribute of everything, then to say of x that it is, is not to say anything to distinguish it from y. To maintain that Pegasus 'is, but does not exist', tells us nothing about Pegasus other than that he does not occupy any spatio-temporal position, something which 'Pegasus does not exist' would alone tell us. If we were to say of numbers, for instance, that they are, but do not exist (= occupy some spatio-temporal position) we would still be left with the problem with which we started out: *what* are they, given that they are not material objects?[4] Only if the concept of being has some specified content can we decide of any given x, whether or not it is: and if some content is specified, then we can say *what* x is and what it is not.

Another suggestion for avoiding the problem of specifying the manner of existence of those things which are said to exist although they do not occupy any spatio-temporal position is what might be characterized as the thesis that everything exists in its own way. Alston advocates such a view in 'The Ontological Argument Revisited'[5] as a means of saving the argument from the hoary objection that existence is not a predicate (since 'Before we can attach any predicate to anything...we must presuppose that it exists'[6]): it is an example of the convolutions which critics feel constrained to perform once they have accepted an entirely irrelevant objection to the argument. Alston propounds a thesis of 'modes of existence'. 'We can', he maintains, 'use one mode of existence to set up the subject, and another mode of existence as the predicate. At least, once we recognise the diverse modes of existence, the standard arguments are powerless to prevent this.'[7] These modes of existence are 'existence in reality', 'existence in fiction', 'existence in myth', etc. Everything exists in some mode or other, so that the apparent problem of referring to non-existents disappears; Pegasus, who exists in myth, does not exist in reality. The proper objection to the ontological argument then becomes this: 'Now it seems to be a defining feature of all nonreal modes of existence that any statement about something which exists in such a mode will have no implications with respect to real things, except for its real correlate and any implications that might have... If the existence of something in one mode should imply its existence in another mode, the distinction between these two modes would crumble.'[8] But the distinction cannot be maintained anyway. Either modes of existence are sorts of existence or they are not. If they are, then we still face the problem of specifying just what existence is, given that it is not occupation of some spatio-temporal position. I see no alternative to some such line as this. For any x, if x is in any mode of existence, then x is; and the unhelpfulness of this has already been made clear. If on the other hand, modes of existence are not sorts of existence, then what are they? Once again, we are left with the difficulty of specifying, with reference to each mode of existence, just what it is to exist in that mode. (If modes of existence are not sorts of existence, then of course it becomes very misleading to say that everything exists, even if this is qualified by 'in its particular mode'.) And if one tries to posit existence in reality as somehow a logically basic mode of existence, from which the other modes get their sense, then the whole point of Alston's scheme is lost, since we would have to specify what it was to exist in reality: either it is to occupy some spatio-temporal position, or it is not. If it is the former, then we have not progressed beyond the original difficulty. If the latter, then again, we must say just what it is.

This is precisely what Quine suggests we do, when he argues that 'exists' does not have spatio-temporal connotations:

> If Pegasus existed, he would indeed be in space and time, but only because the word 'Pegasus' has spatio-temporal connotations, and not because 'exists' has spatio-temporal connotations. If spatio-temporal reference is lacking when we affirm the existence the cube root of 27, this is simply because a cube root is not a spatio-temporal kind of thing, and not because we are being ambiguous in our use of 'exists'.[9]

Everything is (something) — but this is trivial. Of those things which exist, come occupy some spatio-temporal position, and others, like numbers and feelings, do not. What it means to say of numbers and feelings that they exist, that they are not fictions, depends on just what it is that numbers and feelings are, what sorts of thing they are. Ideas, for instance, may be said to exist; the idea of space-travel existed long before space-travel became technically possible. Someone had such an idea. Granted that ideas are invented and not discovered, so that, in my terminology, ideas are fictions, we see that fictions too exist. What that means, however, is that they are created and sustained by people — just the opposite of what it means to say of three-toed sloths, for instance, that they exist. This view is in fact not so very different from Alston's; it is less systematic, however, and also clearer about what it is that determines the nature of a 'mode' of existence, namely the thing which exists in that particular way. Some things, then, do not exist, although the idea of them exists: Pegasus, unicorns, etc. And yet, since Pegasus and unicorns *are* ideas — for they do not exist — they too exist! The point is, of course, that in saying 'Pegasus does not exist', one means that Pegasus, who might be thought to be a horse, is in fact an idea and not a horse at all. It is the *context* which enables us to avoid the apparent puzzle about referring to non-existents. To say that Pegasus does not exist is to regard Pegasus as at least a candidate for a particular sort of existence; and that in turn is to have a notion of what sort of thing Pegasus would be if he actually existed. To say that he does not in fact exist is to say that Pegasus, being what he is, is not that sort of thing after all, namely, not a horse-like animal. He is a fiction. And fictions, although they may exist inasmuch as they are created and sustained, do not exist in the way that animals exist. When asking whether Pegasus existed, we thought it possible that Pegasus might be a species of animal; now we find he is not, so we say he does not exist. If x is a member of the class of fictions, then x does not exist. The class of fictions itself, however, does exist, which is to say that it is a coherent (possible) idea which has been conceived. It may even be that the idea of a square circle exists, since for an incoherent idea to exist, it need only be mentioned; *that* is what it is — all it is — for an incoherent idea to exist.

I seem now to be in a position disturbingly similar to Alston's. Of course we are quite at liberty to maintain that everything exists in some way or another, since everything *is* something or other; whereas some things do not exist inasmuch as they are not in fact the sort of thing which they are posited as being. But although this seems true, it is unhelpful. It is particularly unhelpful when it is remembered that I started out by suggesting that to say that x exists is to assert that x is not a fiction (p. 70). This now turns out to be the case only where 'x' is something which has been posited as non-fictional, something which was thought possibly to be a non-fiction. Unless Quine's thesis is to collapse into Alston's,[10] he must be understood as saying that 'x exists' means 'x is indeed the sort of thing it was taken possibly to be when the question of its existence arose'.

The point is, it seems to me, that questions of the existence of things come up just in those cases where we are wondering whether or not the thing in question is a fiction: where we know already that x is a fiction (as in the case of Pegasus) we do not ask whether it exists. Furthermore, 'exists' very often does have spatio-temporal connotations. But this is unsurprising, since the underlying assumption of most contemporary western thought is that reality is exclusively spatio-temporal, or material; that the contrary of 'x is a fiction' is 'x occupies some spatio-temporal position', or 'x is a material object'.

There are of course problem cases, where there is uncertainty about whether or not to say of something that it exists — and these are just those cases which might be thought to suggest that reality is not exclusively spatio-temporal. Perhaps consideration of the following two examples might help in seeing just why discussion of the ontological argument so often becomes tied up with discussions of various doctrines about what it means to say of something that it exists.

Consider Joan, a spiritualist, who believes that beings survive their death in some non-physical form. One can imagine her recounting the following tale. 'My grandfather died in 1968 and for the first few years he used to get in touch with me quite often. But then, about ten years after he passed over, his communications became less frequent, until I hardly ever used to hear from him. In early February 1979, the messages became very faint, and I haven't heard from him since October 23rd, 1979. He must have crossed over onto the next plane, where I'm sure we'll all meet up again at some point. And of course we'll meet in spirit, not in body; that's the joy of it.' No doubt not all spiritualists would be happy with all of this monologue, and of course it raises all sorts of philosophical problems. However, it at least affords an opportunity to ask how someone like Joan would respond to the question, So you think your grandfather still exists? Whether there is an orthodox spiritualist view on this I do not know; but I think we may imagine Joan replying either affirmatively or negatively. If she agrees that her grandfather still exists, then clearly she does not mean by 'he still exists' that he still occupies some spatio-temporal position. His body, that part of him which once was in space and time, is dead: it is his spirit which still exists. And a person's spirit, since it is not a material entity, does not occupy any spatio-temporal position. Thus, if Joan agrees that her grandfather still exists, she is committed to using 'exists' without any spatio-temporal connotation. Such a commitment, I suggest, would arise from a conviction that it is extremely odd to deny that something real does not exist. Joan thinks that it is not the case that her grandfather, considered as a currently living being, is a fiction; thus she says that he (still) exists. On the other hand however, she may deny that her grandfather still exists, precisely because saying that he exists would carry the suggestion of continuing spatio-temporal position, which is of course something she wants to deny. It is clear that this does not in any way modify her conviction that her grandfather, considered as a currently living being, if not a fiction. Thus 'exists' does not in all contexts have a clearly unambiguous one.

Another area where similar difficulties arise is of course Plato's Theory of Forms itself. Are we to believe that the Forms exist? Vlastos suggests we should not, because existence-statements have spatio-temporal connotations:

> ...it may be worth pointing out that in contexts where his need to express existence in our common use of the term...is most urgent he [Plato] tends to eke out 'to be' with locatives: 'it makes no difference whether it (the Ideal State) exists *somewhere* or will exist...'(*Rep*. 592b); we should not fear that the soul may be dissipated at death, 'vanishing into thin air and existing *nowhere*' (...*Phdo*. 84b, Hackforth's translation).[11]

He writes further:

> As we commonly use the word 'existence', degrees of it (as distinct from degrees of perfection of things in existence) makes no sense whatever; the idea of one individual existing more, or less, than another would be a rank absurdity...Would anyone seriously suggest that Plato wants to undermine our faith in the existence of the beds we sleep in, buy and sell, etc., when he compares their 'being' unfavourably with that of their Form in *Rep.* X? His contention that they are not 'really real' surely *presupposes* their existence.[12]

But if the Forms do not exist, although they are real — more real than things which do exist — then the nature of reality is not exclusively spatio-temporal. However, this leaves one wondering just *how* one is to think of the Forms, entities which are real, but which cannot be said to exist. The temptation is to think of them as concepts; and then it would be odd, for us if not for Plato, to say that they are more real than physical objects, since the idea of concepts not dependent for their being on the human mind is, to say the least, difficult. This may be the thinking behind Grube's conviction that '...to look upon the Ideas as concepts in any shape or form is a mistake, for a concept cannot by definition exist until the mind has conceived it, and this Plato quite deliberately refused to admit of his Ideas. They are rather the objective reality to which the concept corresponds, and they exist whether we know them or not. If the whole human race were senseless savages, the eternal Form of Justice would exist as fully in any case, though it would be even less perfectly realized in the world.'[13] However, if the 'eternal Form of Justice' is not an entity occupying some spatio-temporal position and not a concept, or not just a concept, then what are we to understand by an affirmation of its existence? Vlastos suggests that 'real' is used by Plato in two senses: 'cognitively dependable, undeceiving'; and a sense 'which becomes most prominent when he thinks of the "really real" things, the Forms, as objects of mystical experience...[a sense in which] the word functions as a value-predicate, but one that transcends the usual specifications of value, moral, aesthetic, and religious...'.[14] This is doubtless correct. Plato's notion of the nature of reality is certainly not spatio-temporal, for the spatio-temporal features of the world are to be located in the second division of knowledge. They are less real than the Forms, which are 'known but not seen'.[15] However, to gloss 'real' by 'cognitively reliable and, in some cases, mystically valuable', leaves something out of account:

> ...the Good not only infuses the power of being known into all things known, but also bestows upon them their being and existence, and yet the Good is not existence, but lies far beyond it in dignity and power. —*Rep.* 509b

The Good is both cognitively reliable and valuable, or rather it is the source of cognitive reliability and of value;[16] but it seems to be more than that. As Russell once said of a universal, 'It is neither in space nor in time, neither material nor mental; yet it is something.'[17] Vlastos's account of how we are to understand the reality of Forms makes them too dependent on us: we find them cognitively reliable and valuable, but what are they? What sort of entity are they — if not concepts invented to solve epistemological and axiological problems? If the nature of reality is defined for Plato solely in terms of value and cognitive reliability, and not in terms of those things which occupy spatio-temporal position, we still want to ask of the most real entities, the Forms, whether or not they exist. If not, then their objectivity and independence of the human mind seems in jeopardy; if they do exist, then *how* do they exist, given that they do not do so in the way that material objects exist?

Now this is just the problem which arises when theologians talk about the existence or otherwise of God. Etienne Gilson, for example, wants to maintain most strongly that God exists:

> Thinkers like Plato and Aristotle, who do not identify God and being, could never dream of deducing God's existence from his idea; but when a Christian thinker like St. Anselm asks himself whether God exists, he asks, in fact, whether Being exists, and to deny God is to affirm that Being does not exist...The inconceivability of the non-existence of God could have no meaning at all save in a Christian outlook where God is identified with being, and where, consequently, it becomes contradictory to suppose that we think of him and think of him as non-existent.[18]

According to Gilson, then, 'Being does not exist' is a contradiction; and God, since he is identified with Being, must therefore exist. Paul Tillich however, takes a contrary view:

> The being of God is being-itself. The being of God cannot be understood as the existence of a being alongside others or above others. If God is *a* being, he is subject to the categories of finitude, especially to space and substance...[Being-itself] stands in contrast to every being. As classical theology has emphasized, God is beyond essence and existence. Logically, being-itself is "before," "prior to," the split which characterizes finite being... Thus the question of the existence of God can be neither asked nor answered. If asked, it is a question about that which by its very nature is above existence, and therefore the answer — whether negative or affirmative — implicitly denies the nature of God. It is as atheistic to affirm the existence of God as it is to deny it. God is being-itself, not *a* being.[19]

For Tillich, then, 'x exists' does not mean the same as it does for Gilson. Gilson, it seems, does not wish to deny existence to anything which is real. When he writes of 'a transcendent God whose pure act of existing is radically distinct from our own borrowed existence',[20] he is presumably prepared to answer the question, 'But how can *both* God and men *exist*?' in these terms: '—even if we cannot imagine supra-temporal or non-temporal existence, we can conceive it by divesting the words that we use of their suggestions of temporality'.[21] He is right, of course, to distinguish being unable to conceive from being unable to imagine; but *can* we conceive of non-spatio-temporal existence by divesting our words of their spatio-temporal suggestions? Tillich would argue not, and that therefore we cannot say of God that he exists.

To return to Anselm's principle that any entity which exists is greater than any entity which is a mere fiction. If existence-statements necessarily have spatio-temporal implications, and there are real things which do not exist, then there are no adequate grounds for holding the principle to be true. For if some real things do not exist, there is no reason to suppose those (real) things which do exist to be ontologically greater than the former; that would be to ascribe ontological supremacy to spatio-temporal entities. But there are no *compelling* reasons for doing so. If, on the other hand, existence-statements necessarily have spatio-temporal connotations, and all real things exist, then the principle is not strictly true. For if reality is wholly spatio-temporal, then spatio-temporal entities are not *more* real than mere fictions;

rather, spatio-temporal entities are real, and fictions are not real. On the materialist view no doctrine of *degrees* of reality is possible. The materialist might modify his position to allow that at least some fictions are real in some sense (i.e., they are objects of experience), but that this sense is different from, and doubtless logically subordinate to, the sense in which spatio-temporal entities are real. He might, that is, be willing to talk of kinds, rather than degrees, of reality — as Vlastos suggests Plato should have done[22] — but even if he is so willing, the assertion of Anselm's principle is not open to him. For he has no means of *comparing* ontologically the status of one kind of reality with another.

Four points emerge from this rather inconclusive discussion. First, to the extent that 'x exists' often implies that x is a spatio-temporal entity, it is because it is commonly assumed that the material world constitutes reality. Second, 'x exists' need not carry such a connotation. As Quine suggests, the ascription of existence to x follows, and cannot precede, a decision as to the sort of thing x is, or is purported to be — otherwise we find ourselves proscribing perfectly good expressions of the form 'x exists'.[23] Third, those concerned with Anselm's argument need have no particular interest in a resolution of the problem of how best to employ the word 'exists' so as to cause least confusion. Anselm is concerned with the question of whether or not there is a God, and when he claims that God exists there is of course no suggestion of 'exists' carrying any spatio-temporal connotation: indeed, chs. V–XXV of the *Proslogion* are largely concerned to explain how properties apparently attributable only to spatio-temporal entities may be attributed to God despite his being non-spatio-temporal. Fourth, it is clear that to posit x as a subject of reference need not be to posit x as existing, or as real; 'x exists' and 'x is real' may therefore be forms of informative proposition, telling us that x is not a fiction, not just a creation of the human mind. Whether or not we wish to say of God that he exists, then, the question at issue is this: is God a fiction or not? The logic of 'exists' has no special relevance for consideration of the ontological argument.

What is necessary is to see what *sort* of thing God might be, if not a fiction. It is because the question of the very possibility of there being such a thing as God does not arise for Anselm that he is able to discuss God's attributes in *Proslogion* III — XXV on the basis of his conclusion in ch. II that God is real. As discussion of 'x exists' makes quite clear however, this is the reverse of the procedure required, since we do not in fact know what sort of thing God is purported to be. Anselm *assumes* his formula to carry the requisite content; but this assumption, a grand metaphysical error, inherited from platonism, which serves to obscure the central problem of the Judaeo-Christian God, is why his argument, although formally valid, fails to establish that God is not a fiction.

In brief, the Judaeo-Christian God cannot be absolutely different in kind from all other things. On the other hand however, if God's reality is not to be entirely different in kind from that of everything else, then it must certainly be of a higher degree than that of anything else (this is of course the point behind Anselm's formula), otherwise God would not be something other than but superior to everything else. Christianity and Platonism have thus in common a basic difficulty, namely that of giving an account of the relation between differences in kind and differences in degree such that x can differ from y on both counts. This is of course what makes the whole notion of a hierarchically structured reality so problematic. In ch. 2 I distinguished two uses of 'reality': (1) to cover all that there is, all the individuals and all the sorts of things there are, fictions as well as non-fictions; and (2) to cover only those things which are ontologically independent of our thought. In the following, I shall refer to these as '$real_1$' or '$reality_1$' and '$real_2$' or '$reality_2$' respectively. Now although it may be intelligible to say that everything there is, is part of reality (= $reality_1$) it is not particularly useful or informative: if this is how 'real' is used, then 'x is real' does not serve to distinguish x from anything else. And of course, the claim that the Forms alone are truly real is made on the basis of '$real_2$'; only the Forms are truly ontologically independent. If, however, the Forms are to be compared with other sorts of entity, then there must be something which they have in common with them, on the basis of which comparison in terms of degree may be made. But nothing else that comprises the ontological scale can be $real_2$, since everything other than the Forms is to a greater or lesser degree ontologically dependent. Nor will reality$_1$ do as a basis for comparison since obviously no degree of reality$_1$ is possible. Everything there is, is something or other *tout court*: there can be no question of x's being a particular sort of thing to a certain degree. Either a unicorn is a mythical creature or it is not. Of course, x may be partly one sort of thing, and partly another — but however many sorts of thing x may partly be, it cannot be any of them to a greater or lesser degree. Whereas it makes perfectly good sense to say that what the abominable snowman is, is comprised partly by 'animal' and partly by 'mythical beast', it makes no sense to say that the abominable snowman's *being* an animal, or his *being* a mythical beast is a matter of degree. The abominable snowman may be several kinds of thing; but, with reference to any one of them, he either is or is not an example thereof. Nor are the sorts of thing designated by 'animal' and 'mythical beast' respectively degrees, either one of another, or of some third sort of thing. If Plato's suggestion that different sorts of thing are objects of knowledge to different degrees is to be intelligible, then necessary knowledge, empirical knowledge and opinion must all be degrees of some one thing, or sort of thing, of which degrees are possible. But there appears to be no candidate for this position. Not all are species of knowledge; nor does there appear to be anything else of which degrees are possible, and of which they are all species. This is of course no more than a brief resumé of a standard criticism of the Theory of Forms. Just as a Form is both an individual and a species of thing, so it is both a member of the class of real things, and the sole sort of thing which is real. Now, Anselm's idea of God, that is the Christian idea of God, faces the same difficulty. Eternal and self-sufficient reality, God's *sort* of reality, is also the highest possible *degree* of reality, a reality which is common to all real things. On the one hand, there are differences in kind between God's sort of reality and all other sorts of reality (or, between the way in which God is real and the ways in which all other things are real): and on the other, God's reality is the highest possible degree of reality. If this is to be intelligible, then there must be some way of achieving a logical reconciliation between these two apparently contradictory claims.

A necessary condition of our intelligibly defining God as the most real entity possible, or the maximally real entity, is that it should be logically possible that God be not a fiction, since, as we have seen, the determination of the ontological status of an entity must be logically prior to the determination of its reality. Or, to put it another way, in order to determine whether the notion of God as the most real entity possible is a coherent one, we must first determine in what God's reality would consist, were he indeed real. If there were such an entity as God, what sort of entity would it be?

The peculiar difficulty of answering this question lies of course in God's uniqueness. One way to bring this out is to consider Aquinas's discussion of Aristotle's 'being through itself'.[24] This idea is used, Aquinas says, to divide being 'into the ten genera'; and when used in this way, '"being" can be said only of something which exists in reality'.[25] If, however, we say, 'God is a real entity', i.e., 'There is a God', or 'Something-or-other has divine attributes', we are not referring to a member of any of the ten genera (or however many genera we may care to posit). We are not saying of 'some kind of objects' that something *is* that sort of thing'. For God is outside all the genera: as Aquinas himself says, 'The act of existing which God is is such that no addition can be made to it. Hence, by its very purity, *this act of existing is distinct from every other act of existing.*'[26] But if God is distinct from every other sort of real entity, then to say that there is a God leaves unanswered this crucial question: What is God? or A real *what* is God? And without an answer to this question, the assertion that there is a God has no clear sense. I am not arguing that we need to know fully what God is (indeed, I defended Anselm against Aquinas on this point in ch. 3) for that is not the case of any entity to which we may legitimately refer; but rather that we must know what sort of entity something is alleged to be before we can ask whether or not it exists. Thus the Thomistic way round this problem fails altogether to meet the point. Consider these remarks of Gilson for example: 'Where existence is alone, as is the case in God, Whose essence is one with His existence, there is no becoming. God is, and, because He is no particular essence, but the pure act of existence, there is nothing which He can become, and all that can be said about Him is, *He Is.*'[27] Whether or not it is legitimate to assert that God cannot become anything, or change in any way, Gilson's grounds for holding that this is the case will not do. What is 'the pure act of existence', and how does it differ from no act of existence at all? If 'He Is' is all that can be said of the nature of God's reality, then the conclusion that 'God' is an incoherent concept becomes very tempting. I shall therefore turn to consider what sort of thing God might be, even though acknowledging that he may be the sole entity which is that sort of thing.

Chapter 5

God and necessary existence

I shall begin by returning to some of the issues discussed in ch. 2. For it is Anselm's claim that God is unable not to exist that provides the best starting-point for a discussion of the nature of God: it is God's inability not to exist which marks off his manner of existence from that of all other existents. In ch. 2 I argued that *Proslogion* III constitutes the beginning of Anselm's discussion of God's nature, which he thinks it a particular virtue of his formula to establish, as well as establishing that there is a God: '...I began to wonder if perhaps it might be possible to find one single argument that for its proof required no other save itself, and that by itself would suffice to prove that God really exists, that He is the supreme good needing no other, and is He whom all things have need of for their being and well-being, and also to prove whatever we believe about the Divine Being' (*Pros.*, Preface, p. 103). Anselm says that we cannot think of God as not existing; and that this is so because God cannot not exist. This latter claim, I argued, does not amount for Anselm to the claim that 'God exists' is a necessary proposition: rather, he understands it as stating that God is eternal and self-sufficient. (I say 'self-sufficient' in preference to 'self-existent' because the latter might be thought, whether mistakenly or not, to carry the suggestion of God's bringing about his own reality, a suggestion which I should prefer to avoid. The notion of an uncreated God seems less problematic than that of a self-created God.)

Now I left unanswered at the end of ch. 2 the crucial question of exactly how we are to understand the claim that, being eternal and self-sufficient, God is unable not to exist; and specifically what the modal status of such a claim might be. For although this is not a question raised by Anselm — the notion of logical necessity is absent from his work — it is central to an understanding of what sort of thing God is. Is it a putative *matter of fact* that God is unable not to exist (unable not to be real, unable to be a fiction) or is this a *logical* claim? The answer to this question clearly has important implications for an investigation of the alleged nature of God: since, if the claim is a logical one, then either God will be a necessarily existent being precisely in the sense which Hume and Kant hold to be a nonsense, or the idea of God is incoherent. Although Anselm himself can offer us no great help here, he does come near to facing this sort of issue in the following passage in *Cur Deus Homo*, and the outcome is interesting:

> And as, when God does a thing, since it has been done, it cannot be undone, but must remain an actual fact; still, we are not correct in saying that it is impossible for God to prevent a past action from being what it is. For there is no necessity or impossibility in the case whatever, but the simple will of God, which chooses that truth should be eternally the same, for he himself is truth. — II, XVIII (a), pp. 273–4[1]

In modern terminology, this would seem to imply that logical laws themselves are dependent on God's will, and that any law of logic is therefore subject to alteration or cancellation at God's behest. Such a view may or may not be intelligible; it would certainly raise grave difficulties for logicians, implying as it does that the truth-values of logical truths could be altered at God's will. Becker's Postulate, for example, would be vitiated by such a view, since it would be merely a contingent matter that 'truth should be eternally the same', a matter contingent on God's choice. However all that may be, what is clear is that there would be little point in the question which one wishes to ask concerning the above quotation: is it a necessary or a contingent truth that 'the simple will of God…chooses that truth be eternally the same'? This is of course just what I wish to ask of God's alleged inability not to be real.

In order to be quite clear how this question arises, I shall refer again to *Reply* I:

> Further: even if it can be thought of, then certainly it necessarily [2] exists. For no one who denies or doubts that there is something than which a greater cannot be thought denies or doubts that, if this being were to exist, it would not be capable of not-existing either actually or in the mind — otherwise it would not be that than which a greater cannot be thought. But, whatever can be thought as existing and does not actually exist, could, if it were to exist, possibly not exist either actually or in the mind. For this reason, if it can be merely thought, 'that than which a greater cannot be thought' cannot not exist. — p. 171

Are we to take this as asserting that God cannot as a matter of fact not-exist, or that he logically cannot not-exist: or, is the proposition, 'God cannot not-exist' a contingent or a necessary proposition? I think it is clear that Anselm's conception of God is such that it implies that God's reality is a matter of necessity, and not contingency. For if 'God cannot not-exist' were a contingent proposition, then it would be logically possible both that it be false, and that, if true, circumstances could so change as to render it false (and vice-versa). Thus it would be logically possible that God *could* not-exist, that is, that God be not real. But if that were the case, then we could think of God as not real. Anselm's view, however, that God is unable not to exist, and that therefore we are unable to think of him as non-existent if we are thinking truly, must ignore the crucial question of the modal status of 'unable' in 'God is unable not to exist', simply because he lacks the modern categories of necessity and contingency. If, however, in an attempt to avoid embroiling Anselm in modal questions, it were claimed that 'God cannot not-exist' is true simply because God, as it happens, cannot not-exist, and that it would become false if circumstances were to change, then that would of course be to concede the contingency of the proposition. And if that were conceded, then again, it would have also to be conceded that 'God cannot be thought not to exist' is false. On the other hand, if it were claimed that circumstances could not change, then we should have to ask whether the force of 'could' here is factual or logical. In short, it is clear that the question of the modal status of assertions of God's reality must be confronted, even though Anselm does not do so.

I shall argue for the implication which I have suggested is to be found in Anselm. That is, given that the concept of

God is that of an eternal, self-sufficient entity, it follows that 'God exists', or 'God is real', is a necessary proposition: since if the truth of the claim that God is unable not to exist were held to be contingent upon empirical facts, events, or states of affairs, then this would contradict the ascription to God of eternity and aseity. The existence of an entity which is held to be eternal and self-sufficient can be dependent only upon logical conditions. To use John Hick's vocabulary, I shall argue, against him, that ontological, or factual, necessity implies logical necessity.[3] This is of course centrally important for the Christian concept of God: and it is a central achievement of Anselm's argument that reflection upon it should uncover the point. Less importantly, though hardly less interestingly, it is this issue which, I suspect, lurks behind much of the argument's uneasily chequered career.

Hume's classical empiricist dictum, that whatever we conceive as existent, we can also conceive as non-existent, seeks of course to preclude such investigation *a priori*. But such issues cannot be decided by *fiat*, not even by Humean *fiat*: here, after all, is a putative counter-example. That its success would overturn a central tenet of empiricism hardly constitutes rational grounds for immediate dismissal of that possibility. John Hick's remark, for example, that 'It is an implication of this contemporary empiricist view of logical necessity as analytic that an existential proposition (i.e., a value of the propositional function "x exists") cannot be logically necessary',[4] while doubtless true, is otiose. There are no *a priori* grounds for supposing that there cannot be any concept logically parallel to those which, like that of a square circle, are 'so badly made,' as R. M. Adams puts it, 'that we can see, just be examining it, that nothing could possibly satisfy it.'[5] No doubt the business of examining "so well made..." a concept would be an indefinitely more complex matter than examining that of a square circle; but mere stipulation that such an enterprise is impossible is no substitute for argument for the truth of the empiricist view. Such argument must take the form of investigating the logical circumstances which arise in the individual case at issue, and not that of a blanket stipulation to which a particular case — by definition unique — is argued to be an exception.

If Anselm's concept of God is indeed by implication that of an entity whose existence is logically necessary, then to what extent may the being he defines as that than which nothing greater can be thought be identified with the Christian God? Hick cites what is doubtless true, that 'nowhere in the biblical thought about God is use made of the idea of logical necessity',[6] as evidence that such identification is illegitimate. But the fact that an idea does not explicitly appear in biblical thought does not show that what does appear does not entail it. Can a Christian accept that it just so happens that there is a God? For if 'God exists', or 'God is real' is a contingent proposition, then if there is indeed a God it is contingently true that there is a God: it could conceivably be the case that there be no God, but it so happens that there is. If, however, it happens to be the case that there is a God, it might, as with all other contingent existents, happen to be the case that there is no God. That is to say, things might be different. This seems to me clearly unacceptable for a Christian. For if he were to take 'There is a God' as a contingent proposition, then he would have to be prepared to accept, for instance, that there may have been a time when there was no God, or that there may come a time when there will no longer be a God. He would have to be prepared to accept that something could occur to render the proposition 'There is a God' false, for this is the mark of contingent existents. But God, unlike any individual item in the universe, surely does not just happen to exist, according to the Christian claim. In this Findlay was clearly right when using the conviction that God's 'non-existence must be wholly unthinkable in any circumstances'[7] as the basis of his alleged disproof of God's existence.

If 'There is a God' is not a contingent proposition, then it must presumably be a necessary proposition, which is what Findlay, Hartshorne, and Malcolm conclude. However, if 'There is a God' is a necessary proposition like other necessary propositions, then well-known problems arise. If analyticity or tautology are taken to be exhaustive of the property of necessity possessed by some propositions, then such propositions are true or false solely in virtue of the meaning of the terms they consist in: 'Triangles have three sides' is a necessary proposition, because by 'triangle' we mean 'three-sided figure'. Necessary truths or falsehoods are true or false by convention, we might say. Necessary propositions are truths or falsehoods merely of logic, or of language. Their application, therefore, is limited to what I have termed fictions, that is, to matters which are creations of the human mind: they have no application to anything which is ontologically independent of human beings. If logical necessity is defined rather more broadly, as the property possessed by some propositions of being *a priori* true or *a priori* false, in order more easily to accommodate such examples as 'Whatever is mauve is extended', or 'Nothing can be puce and orange all over at the same time', then it is not immediately clear that this is the case. There are at least *prima facie* grounds for supposing, for example, that 'Whatever is mauve is extended' tells us something about the world, as well as about our use of concepts, that it is an instance of a synthetic *a priori* proposition. Without seeking to contribute to the settlement of this issue, however, I think it clear that such an analysis is limited to very general propositions involving the sort of fundamental categories of thought identified by Kant. Such propositions, therefore, would seem to be at least as much about our thinking as about the world, inasmuch as no empirical evidence could count for or against their truth. Whether one takes a broader or a narrower view of the nature of the necessity attaching to certain propositions, then, it would seem that 'The question is, does the man who worships God believe Him to exist in the way numbers, concepts, or laws of nature exist, or rather in the way a gold miner believes gold to exist in a mine on which he has spent his last cent...?'[8] It is precisely the former sorts of things, which can be the subject of necessary propositions, from which the Christian attempts to distinguish God.

It might be thought, then, that 'God is real' is neither a contingent proposition, nor a necessary one; that God's existence is neither like the existence of empirical entities, nor like that of ideas. The former, propositional, claim appears odd, not to say paradoxical; but the latter claim, about the nature of God's reality, has not the same peculiarity. After all, that is just the point about God — he is like nothing else. But as I have emphasised earlier, the matter cannot be left there, since, if all we can say about God is that he is quite unlike anything else, we cannot begin to answer the question of his existence. What we clearly do know about God, both from the biblical tradition and from Anselm, is that he is an eternal, self-sufficient being.

I showed in ch. 2 why Anselm considers that God must be eternal and self-sufficient: eternity and self-sufficiency are the marks of ontological independence. Since the supreme Nature does not derive its existence from anything, Anselm writes in the *Monologion*, and 'has a beginning neither through nor from itself...nor from nothing, it assuredly has no beginning at all. But neither will it have an end. For, if it is to have an end, it is not supremely immortal and supremely incorruptible.' (ch. XVIII, pp. 68–9) Having shown why God cannot be thought of as being in any time or place, he goes on to explain 'How [he] is better understood to exist *always* than *at every time*', for since God 'is immutable and without parts...is not therefore the term which seems to mean *all time* more properly understood, when applied to this Substance, to signify eternity, which is never unlike itself, rather than a changing succession of times, which is ever in some sort unlike itself?' (ch. XXIV, pp. 82–3) Since God is self-sufficient, he is eternal; he can neither begin nor cease to be what he is. This is not to be understood as meaning that God's reality is everlasting or interminable, but rather that it is outside time altogether, since the passage of time implies the possibility of change. Just this possibility, however, the possibility of real, i.e., empirical change, is what Anselm wishes to deny. This is surely part of the traditional Christian concept of God, derived from a combination of Judaic and Greek ideas. Whatever the philosophical objections of Hartshorne and other process philosophers who want to replace this idea with a concept of God as subject in some ways at least to real change, i.e., to contingency, it would surely not do for one adhering to the traditional Christian concept of God to deny eternity and self-sufficiency of him. On this at least there is agreement among those, shortly to be discussed, who are divided about the relationship between the claim that God is eternal and self-sufficient, and the claim that 'God is real' is a necessary proposition.

I shall mostly confine myself to the notion of eternity, since the substance of the claims that God is eternal and that he is self-sufficient seem the same: both imply that God is ontologically independent, and that is the nub of the argument.[9] Now, it is clear that 'It is necessarily true that God is real' implies 'God is eternal and self-sufficient'. For if God were in time, it would make sense to ask questions about the time before he came to be, and a possible time after he might cease to be: and if God's coming to be were caused by something, his reality would be a dependent reality. But then it would be logically possible that some event or state of affairs should bring about an end to, or have prevented the beginning of, his reality — in which case 'God is real' could not be a necessary proposition. (Nor, of course, as Anselm says in *Reply* I, can it be true of something which is not eternal that it cannot be thought not to exist.) To say of an entity that it necessarily exists is to say that nothing that could occur could have any bearing on the truth of the proposition in question: it could not come about, therefore, that the entity does not exist. Nor can there have been a time when it did not exist. But if there can have been no time at which an (existing) entity did not exist, nor a future time at which it will not exist, then that entity is eternal. That is to say, it is not in time at all, so that nothing that could occur (and whatever occurs, occurs in time) could either initiate or terminate its existence.

What is of greater concern, however, is whether a proposition asserting the existence of an eternal entity must be a necessary proposition. For if so, then given that God is eternal, the proposition 'God is real' must be necessary, with the result that God is a necessary being in just that sense to which Hume and Kant so strongly object. It is of course this question which is so prominent in the debate between Hartshorne and Malcolm and their opponents about the soundness or otherwise of Anselm's so-called second argument: the nature of God's existence is such, Hartshorne and Malcolm maintain, that it could not be asserted in a contingent proposition.

The question then is this: does 'God is eternal' imply '"God is real" is a necessary proposition'? Hartshorne's view, implicit in all his work on the ontological argument, is that God's reality must be necessary,[10] since, 'were God to exist, yet his non-existence to be conceivable, he would either exist by sheer chance or luck, or else owing to some cause';[11] and since he is eternal it cannot be the case that he exists by sheer chance or luck, or else owing to some cause. That he exists, then, must be the case necessarily and not contingently. It is Malcolm, however, who argues explicitly that 'from the supposition that it could happen that God did not exist it would follow that, if He existed, He would have mere duration and not eternity':[12] or at least, he explicitly moves from the ascription to God of eternity, to the ascription to God of necessary existence:

> If God, a being a greater than which cannot be conceived, does not exist then He cannot *come* into existence. For if He did He would either have been *caused* to come into existence or have *happened* to come into existence, and in either case He would be a limited being...If He does exist He cannot have come into existence (for the reasons given), nor can He cease to exist, for nothing could cause Him to cease to exist nor could it just happen that He ceased to exist. So if God exists His existence is necessary.[13]

Malcolm seems simply to take it for granted that the existence of an eternal entity could not be asserted in a contingent proposition, rather than offering any thorough-going argument. This is, I think, understandable, since there *appears* very little to be said. If God is eternal, then he is outside time, in the sense that his existence is not in any way dependent on anything that may happen, or may have happened. Whatever happens, happens in time. Therefore there can be nothing on which God's existence is contingent. Therefore his existence must be necessary.[14] On the face of it, the argument seems quite conclusive. Yet few writers accept it.

In the replies which Malcolm's article elicited, the objection is made, in a variety of ways, that 'for all that he has shown us, it could still be just a fact that God eternally is'.[15] Penelhum continues:

> For one thing, if eternal being were by that very fact also logically necessary being, then, since presumably logically necessary being is unique, there could be no eternal created beings. In any case it seems to cry out for demonstration that nothing can be eternally just so. (Of course, it may be a logical truth that if anything is a property of God it is eternally a property of Him; but this does not tell us whether there is a being to whom such properties eternally belong.)[16]

But the argument given above implies just this, that there can indeed be no eternal created beings, since, if something has been created, it must have been created at a particular time, and can therefore not be eternal — there is a time, the time preceding the moment of its creation, when it did not exist. The medieval view that there are created eternal things, such as the stars, which can nevertheless be thought not to exist,[17] is surely unacceptable on these very grounds. Since the stars are created things, they cannot be eternal.

Plantinga argues in a similar vein in his reply to Malcolm:

(a) N(God never has and never will begin to exist).

(b) N(God never has and never will cease to exist).

(2a) God exists — antecedent of (2) [(2) = 'If God exists, His existence is logically necessary.']

Therefore

(2c) N(God exists) — consequent of (2).

Once again it is apparent that (2c) does not follow from (a), (b), and (2a). What does follow is:

(2c') God always has existed and always will exist.

To put it differently, (a) and (b) together entail the following necessary conditional:

(2') N(If at *any* time God exists, then at *every* time God exists).

If God cannot (logically) come into or go out of existence, it is a necessary truth that if He ever exists, He always exists. But it does not follow that if He exists, the proposition "God exists" is necessary.[18]

But on what is the truth of (2c') contingent? If God always has existed and always will exist, then haow can 'God exists' be a contingent proposition, given that nothing could, logically could, occur to render it false (since God is eternal and self-sufficient)? *How* could it 'just happen(s) that God always has and always will exist (and so happen(s) neither to begin nor cease existing, nor [be] caused either to begin or cease existing)'?[19] Further on, Plantinga produces an uncharacteristically sloppy argument against 'the supposition that God merely happens to exist'[20] entailing 'that "God will cease to exist" is sensible (proposition (b))'.[21] Given that God is eternal, he argues, 'it obviously will not "make sense" to suppose that God will cease to exist',[22] since that would entail that 'There is a time at which God exists, and a later time at which He does not',[23] a proposition which is contradictory. 'Hence the supposition that God merely happens to exist does not entail (b).'[24] But of course that is only to repeat the assumption that God's eternal existence may be asserted in a contingent proposition: it could equally well be said that since 'the supposition that God merely happens to exist' *does* entail (b), a proposition which entails a contradictory proposition, the supposition in question must be false. And, presumably, if the supposition that God may merely happen to exist is false, then 'God exists' cannot be a contingent proposition. The underlying point is that there can be no *empirical* conditions to which 'if' might refer in Plantinga's (2') or in Malcolm's (2); for if there *were* such, then, if God existed, his existence would be dependent, and if he did not exist his nonexistence would be similarly dependent — but this is just what is ruled out by his being unable '(logically) [to] come into or go out of existence'. And if there merely *could be* empirical conditions to which 'if' might refer, then God's existence or nonexistence *could be* dependent; in which case he *might be* logically unable to come into or go out of existence. But again, logical truths are not logical truths contingently: the conditions governing 'might' would have to be logical conditions.[25] This is true also of the conditions to which Plantinga's and Malcolm's 'if's' refer. Such conditions must be logical conditions.

John Hick's objections are in similar vein, but developed in greater detail; and as they are typical of arguments against the move from eternity and aseity to logical necessity I shall concentrate my fire on them. Having cited God's aseity as the logical source of his eternity, and described this as 'something quite different from the distinctively modern thought of "God exists" as a logically necessary truth', namely 'the essence of the (contrasting) notion of God as sheer ultimate, unconditoned reality, without origin or end',[26] that is, of God as a necessary being, which 'sense of ontological or factual necessity'[27] he distinguishes from logical necessity, he continues:

> Again, to refer back to Findlay's discussion, it is meaningless to say of the self-existent being that he might not have existed or that he merely happens to exist...There is no conceivable event such that if it had occurred, or failed to occur, a self-existent being would not have existed; for the concept of aseity is precisely the exclusion of such dependence.[28]

If it is indeed meaningless to say of the self-existent being that he merely happens to exist, then, surely, to hold that

'God exists' is a contingent proposition is mistaken: if it cannot, logically cannot, be the case that God *merely happens* to exist, then it must be the case that God either does not and cannot exist, or exists and cannot but exist. There are no other possibilities. Elsewhere, Hick objects to the contrast between happening to exist and existing necessarily: 'But Findlay, after ruling out the notion of necessary existence, in relation to which alone the contrasting idea of "merely happening to exist" has any meaning, continues to use the latter category...'.[29] If the notion of necessary existence is rejected on empiricist grounds, however, as in Hick's case, then it is rejected precisely because it is an empiricist tenet that, for any x, if x exists, it is possible that something-or-other should bring it about that x does not exist (or have brought it about that x did not exist). That is to say, for any x, if x exists, then it so happens that x exists — it could be, or could have been, otherwise. Surely Hick does not intend to suggest that this tenet, on which he bases his rejection of 'necessary existence' is meaningless? Of course 'merely happening to exist'[30] does not, for an empiricist, stand 'in contrast to some other mode of existing':[31] rather the notion of existence is held not to be capable of having necessary application, in contrast to other ideas (e.g. roundness, triangularity) which are held to be so capable. The distinction remains, whatever one's view of one of its constituent parts.

'The existence of God is either logically necessary or logically impossible' is a dilemma which has no substance, Hick maintains, in criticism of Malcolm's argument.[32] And yet he goes on to say that Anselm proves in *Reply* I that 'God is not nonexistent-but-capable-of-existing, that is, that he is not contingently nonexistent':[33] and that he proves 'that God is not a contingent being, or more precisely that he does not contingently not-exist'.[34] But clearly if God is not a contingent being, then this remains the case whether or not he exists; and so God's existence is logically necessary whether or not he exists. The crucial point which appears to have misled Hick, as it has many other commentators in this area is the need to distinguish logical necessity from logically necessary truth. 'Triangles have three sides' is both a logically necessary proposition and true; it is necessarily true. 'Triangles have seven sides', however, while a logically necessary proposition, is false; it is necessarily false. Similarly, to argue that 'God exists' is a necesssary proposition is not thereby to argue that it is a necessarily true proposition. Its modal status is one thing, its truth-value quite another.[35] Thus the dilemma to which Hick refers appears to him to have no substance because his formulation of it conceals this distinction: as it stands, one of its horns, 'The existence of God is logically necessary...', concerns the modal status of propositions asserting God's existence or nonexistence; whereas the other, 'The existence of God is...logically impossible', concerns also their truth-value. I suspect it may be the ambiguity of 'logically necessary' which has contributed to the confusion here. For 'logically necessary' may be the opposite *either* of 'logically impossible' (necessarily instantiated, as opposed to necessarily uninstantiated) *or* of '(logically) contingent' (instantiable necessarily, as opposed to instantiable contingently). Only in the former use is there a truth-claim. The dilemma is in fact this. Either 'God exists' is necessarily (logically) true or it is necessarily (logically) false. 'Given this concept of an ontologically necessary being [a being who exists eternally and *a se*],' Hick writes, 'it is a matter of logic that if there is such a being, his existence is necessary in the sense that he cannot cease to exist, and that if there is no such being, none can come to exist'.[36] But this is wrong: it is a matter of logic that whether or not there actually is such a being, his existence is necessary and not contingent — that is, if 'God exists' is true, then it is necessarily true, and if false, then necessarily false. At the very end of this paper, Hick appears very nearly to see just this point: 'In being other than a nonexistent-which-might-exist, he [God] *either* exists *or* is a nonexistent which could not exist (i.e., whose existence is impossible). But what is not proved is that he exists.'[37] Quite so. But if God *could* be a nonexistent which could not exist, then he *could* be such that the modal status of propositions asserting his existence or nonexistence were necessary and not contingent. And if he could be such an entity, then he *is* such an entity (again, by Becker's Postulate). In that case however, he cannot be an entity whose existence is a contingent matter. To put it another way; if it is possible that it is necessarily false that God exists, then it cannot be also possible that it is contingently true that he exists. If, as Hick admits Anselm to have proved, God 'does not contingently not-exist', then either his existence is logically impossible (it is necessarily true that he does not exist) or it is logically necessary (it is necessarily true that he exists); that is, either 'God' is necessarily *uninstantiated* or 'God' is necessarily *instantiated*. What is ruled out is just what Hick's unqualified '...he *either* exists...' suggests, namely the possibility that 'God' should be contingently instantiated.

Hick is in fact quite clear that '...it is by definition impossible for an eternal being to cease to exist. If there were an eternal being, its nonexistence would in that case be impossible'[38] since 'There is no conceivable event such that if it had occurred, or failed to occur, a self-existent being would not have existed; for the concept of aseity is precisely the exclusion of such dependence. There is and could be nothing that would have prevented a self-existent being from coming to exist, for it is meaningless even to speak of a self-existent being as *coming* to exist.'[39] Now of course Hick is right that it does not follow from this that there is such a being. The point is, however, that if the nonexistence of an eternal, self-existent being were logically impossible, as Hick agrees is the case, then the modal status of a proposition asserting the existence of such a being would be necessary. And if it is possible that the modal status of such a proposition be necessary, then, again, its modal status is necessary. Precisely because an eternal self-sufficient being cannot, logically, be dependent for its existence on any contingent event or state of affairs, as Hick recognizes, the proposition asserting its existence or nonexistence cannot depend on any contingent conditions for its truth-value; and this makes its modal status necessary, and not contingent. Either it is logically necessary that God exists or it is logically impossible that he exist: 'God exists' is either necessarily true or necessarily false. And this follows from God's eternity and self-sufficiency.

Hick's final objection to deriving logically necessary from eternal existence is that 'it is possible to conceive of something existing eternally, not because it is such that there is and could be no power capable of abolishing it, but only because, although there are powers capable of abolishing it, they always refrain from doing so. Such a being would be eternal by courtesy of the fact that it is never destroyed, but not by the positive virtue or power of being indestructible.'[40]

An eternal being, then, need not be a logically necessary entity. But this will quite clearly not do. Do these powers simply happen always to refrain from exercising their destructive capabilities? If so, then it is logically possible that they should one day exercise them and duly abolish God. Such abolition would, presumably, take place in time. But then, if God could be abolished in time, he cannot be an eternal entity — as Hick himself points out, an eternal being cannot cease by definition to exist. If its not ceasing to exist is merely a contingent matter, then it is not eternal at all, but merely everlasting. It is not that God does not, as it happens, cease to exist: it is logically impossible that he should cease to exist. The positing of powers which happen to withold their prerogative to destroy God is self-contradictory. Curiously, Hick fails to see the self-contradiction even though pointing out in continuation of the passage quoted above that '...it is surely integral to the monotheistic concept of God that God, as the ultimate Lord of all, is not capable of being destroyed'.[41] If it is a logical truth that God is not capable of being destroyed, then it must be a logical truth that there could be no power capable of abolishing him. (To argue that their witholding their prerogative is a matter of necessity, that the powers in question do not just happen to refrain from destroying God, would of course be to concede this point immediately.)

In recognizing that it is logically the case that there cannot be powers which could destroy an eternal self-sufficient entity Hick himself shows what is wrong with his view that 'From the concept of God as ontologically necessary we can derive the analytic truth that if God exists, he exists eternally and *a se*...',[42] but that his existence is nevertheless not a matter of logic. The conditions to which 'if' refers here must be logical conditions (as with Plantinga above) otherwise it would be a matter of fact and not of logic that God was not destroyed; and this is just what Hick, rightly, rules out. If the conditions governing God's existence or non-existence were factual, then Hick's view would be simply self-contradictory, since such conditions can-logically-govern the existence or nonexistence only of those entities which are neither eternal nor self-sufficient: that is precisely what it means to deny that they are such, just as it is precisely what it means to ascribe eternality and self-sufficiency to God to say that his existence or nonexistence does not depend on any empirical conditions.[43]

The nub of the argument against my view is, I suspect, the existence of apparently eternal entities whose existence is nevertheless not logically necessary. This is how Abelson argues:

> Atemporality and aspatiality apply just as well to rules, concepts, propositions, laws of nature, meanings, space-time slabs, and other abstract entities whose existence is clearly *not* necessary. Thus to say that God is eternal, in the sense of atemporality and aspatiality, does not entail that His existence is necessary in any but a Pickwickian sense of "necessary", any more than the atemporal existence of the law of nature that copper conducts electricity entails the necessity of the law.[44]

There are some complex issues here. Firstly, it is not at all clear that rules, concepts, propositions, laws of nature, meanings, and space-time slabs do exist atemporally. Rather, inasmuch as they are abstract entities, it seems to me that they do exist in time — rules, propositions, concepts and meanings (leaving aside laws of nature and space-time slabs for the moment) are all invented, or created entities. That is, they are products of the human mind, or, as I have been using the term, fictions. In the case of any particular example of one of these, there was a time when it did not exist, and there may well come a time when it no longer exists. Rules, concepts, propositions, and meanings all come into and go out of existence; in that sense, therefore, their existence is not atemporal. To say this is not to say that their existence is the same sort of existence as that of other temporal entities, for instance material objects, but merely to point out that although atemporality may *apply* to them, that is not the same as saying that their *existence* is atemporal. Some rules may be thought to apply at any and every time; a concept may fall into disuse, but be ever capable of resurrection; the truth-value of propositions may be unchangeable; once established, meanings, like concepts, may be ever capable of resuscitation. At least, that is the sort of thing I suppose the claim that atemporality applies to these entities amounts to. I certainly do not see what else the claim might mean, other than that they neither come into nor go out of existence; but then the claim would be simply false. These entities, like material objects, are all *made* in some way, and therefore must exist in time. Laws of nature and space-time slabs may be like the others in Abelson's list in this respect. On the other hand, they may be thought to exist independently of their being conceived, to be non-fictional entities. I do not wish to arbitrate between these views here. However, if they are non-fictional entities, then certainly they would seem to be eternal, in the sense that there never was a time when they did not exist, nor can there ever be a time when they will no longer exist. Nor is their existence necessary, since things could have been otherwise; copper might not have conducted electricity. (It might be argued that, even if laws of nature and space-time slabs are not human creations, nevertheless they cannot just be; someone or something must have created them. If that is the case, and they are for instance God's creations, then, being creations, they do not exist eternally. Penelhum's objection to the impossibility of eternal created entities, as I argued above, has little force.)

Laws of nature and space-time slabs might, then, be examples of eternally, but not necessarily, existent entities. Even if self-sufficiency, which seems to me the logical basis of eternity, were brought in here in an attempt to reinforce the case against contingently existing eternal entities, the problem would remain. Laws of nature and space-time slabs cannot be self-sufficient: they cannot have within their own being the ground of their existence. This would certainly be true given the assumption that everything there is, except God himself, is his creation; but of course the view that laws of nature, space-time slabs, the universe itself, etc., just happen to exist is a rejection of that very assumption. The whole notion of inquiring into the grounds of the existence of these sorts of things may be regarded as a — perhaps theologically based — mistake. Abelson's counter-examples cannot be disposed of by insisting that they are not examples of eternally existing entities. Furthermore, other entities may join the list: 'for all we know, certain elementary physical particles — for example, electrons — may always have existed, in which case they surely don't depend upon anything for coming into existence. And for all we know there may be nothing upon which they depend for their continued existence.'[45] If electrons have always existed, and do not depend on anything for their continued existence, it is puzzling to think on what the proposition 'Electrons exist' could be contingent, just as it is puzzling to think on what the proposition 'Copper conducts electricity' is contingent if the relevant law of nature exists eternally and is non-fictional. (It may of course be the case that electrons, like laws of nature, are fictions, and that this is true of *all* the possible counter-examples.[46] But that seems too slender a thread on which to hang the case.) And yet 'Electrons do not exist', like 'Copper does not conduct electricity', certainly does not *seem* to be a necessary proposition, as Plantinga points out.[47] What one may ask, however, is this: on what is it contingent that electrons depend on nothing for their coming into and continuing in existence? Or to put it another way, on what is it contingent that electrons (or laws of nature, or space-time slabs) are the sort of thing they are? A not very helpful answer to both questions is this: these facts are contingent on things being as they are. Since things might have been otherwise the proposition asserting the existence of electrons is a contingent one. Again, I am not at all happy about this, since there seems at least a *prima facie* case that, if things were other than they are, in such a way as to alter the manner of existence of electrons, etc., so that they did depend for their coming into and going out of existence on other entities, then they would not be the sort of thing they are (assuming that they do exist eternally). That is to say that eternal existence can be ascribed only necessarily, since, if it were contingently true that x is eternal, then it would be possible that x should cease to be eternal — but then x would not be eternal at all (see p. 99). And if 'x exists eternally' must be a necessary proposition, then so must 'x exists' — since the former implies the latter — in which case eternal existence can be ascribed only to those entities whose existence is logically necessary. There can be no contingently existing eternal entity. This would imply that either electrons exist necessarily, or they are fictions (more explicitly, explanatory hypotheses).

However, even if I am wrong about this there would seem nonetheless to be a difference between God and electrons, etc., which would dispose of the latter as counter-examples to the thesis that if God exists eternally, the proposition asserting his existence is necessary and not contingent. In the case of God, but not in the case of electrons, etc., it is necessarily true that he is eternal. God's eternity, his being the sort of thing he is, is not contingent on things being as they are. Whereas the eternity of electrons is contingent on things being as they are, so that the proposition 'Electrons exist' is a contingent proposition, the eternity of God is not contingent on anything, so that the proposition 'God exists' cannot be contingent. Plantinga notes this point: Malcolm may have had in mind, he writes, that 'the assertion that God does not depend upon anything is necessary. And it is inconsistent to hold both that God's existence is contingent and that it is a necessary truth that He depends upon nothing at all either for coming into or for continuing in existence... But I must confess inability to see the inconsistency.'[48] If, however, 'God is eternal' is a necessary truth, and it is therefore logically impossible that God should depend upon anything for coming into or continuing in existence, then, again, on what could the truth or falsity of the proposition 'God exists' be contingent? Whereas in the case of, say, electrons, the truth or falsity of the proposition asserting their existence is contingent on how things are (even if it is the case that electrons exist eternally) in the case of God, the truth or falsity of 'God exists' is not so contingent. That, surely, is the point of insisting that it is necessarily, and not contingently, true that God is eternal. In contradistinction to Plantinga, I must confess that I am unable to see how 'God exists' could be a contingent proposition given the necessary truth of 'God is eternal'.

An immediate objection is that, if 'God exists' is a necessary proposition, then its denial must be self-contradictory — but surely one cannot convict of self-contradiction all those who deny and have denied that there is a God. Yet it is precisely this which Anselm does in *Proslogion* II — IV. The Fool is able to deny God's existence only because he fails to realise that to do so is self-contradictory. And yet this is not to say that it is necessarily true that God exists. The failure of Hartshorne and Malcolm to maintain a distinction between necessary status and necessary truth in their arguments seems to be the seed of much of the subsequent confused argument about the modal status of 'God exists'. They both object to the proposition, 'If God exists, then he necessarily exists', on the grounds that the antecedent clause implies that it is possible that God does not exist, which would contradict the subsequent clause, one which excludes that very possibility.

But this is a confusion. Clearly, the modal status of 'God exists' cannot depend upon the truth or falsity of 'God exists', as it would seem to be held to depend by those who propose that if God exists, he necessarily exists. But surely no one claims *that*. It is the *truth* of 'God necessarily exists', and not its modal status, which is held to depend on the truth or falsity of 'God exists'. This becomes clearer if the proposition which Hartshorne and Malcolm take to be self-contradictory is filled out: 'If God exists, then it is necessarily true that he exists.' The point is that, contrary to Malcolm, those who maintain this proposition to be true do not (or should not) 'agree that the proposition "God necessarily exists" is an a priori truth'.[49] It is an *a priori* proposition, and as such, may be either an *a priori* truth or an *a priori* falsehood. And whether it is the former or the latter depends on the truth or falsity of 'God exists'. Its being *a priori*, as opposed to contingent, depends on the sort of existence which is being ascribed to God, which in turn depends on the sort of entity God is thought to be. Furthermore, there is clearly a condition available for the antecedent clause of the proposition 'If God exists, then it is necessarily true that he exists' – namely the coherence or otherwise of 'God'. If God exists, and whether he does or not depends on whether or not it is possible that he exist, which in turn depends on the coherence or otherwise of the concept of God, then the truth that he exists is a necessary truth; if the concept of God is incoherent, so that it is impossible that God exist, then the proposition 'God exists' is a necessary falsehood.[50]

Consider the following modal argument:
(1) God is eternal (by definition).
(2) For any x, if x is eternal, then 'x exists' is a necessary proposition (from the argument above).
(3) Therefore 'God exists' is a necessary proposition.
(4) Thus, 'God exists' is either necessarily true or necessarily false.
(5) If 'God exists' is not necessarily false, it is necessarily true.
(6) Thus, if it is possible that 'God exists' is true, then it is necessarily true; that is, if 'God exists' is a coherent proposition, then it is a necessarily true proposition.
(7) Therefore, if it is possible that God exists, then he (necessarily) exists.

That, however, is as far as the argument can take us: (3) does not imply anything at all about the truth-value of 'God exists', but only something about its modal status. Anselm takes it for granted that it is possible that there be a God; Hartshorne maintains that it is intuitively true (although he argues also that 'The only logically admissable way to reject theism is to reject the very idea of God as either contradictory or empty of significance'[51]); and Malcolm maintains it need not be demonstrated, since he suspects that 'the argument can be thoroughly understood only by one who has a view of that "form of life" that gives rise to the idea of an infinitely great being, who views it from the *inside*...'.[52] What needs to be done is to investigate whether it is possible that there be a God. If it is possible, then it is necessarily true that God exists, for, as Aristotle has it, in the case of eternal things, what may be must be:[53] and this itself is the first item of information to be noted in pursuing that investigation. God is that sort of entity which exists necessarily, or is necessarily real, the sort of entity the existence or nonexistence of which is established solely by an inquiry into the *possibility* of its existence.

This is in fact what I take to be the major philosophical achievement of Anselm's argument. In excluding the possibility of a logically possible, but fictional, eternal and self-sufficient entity, it shows that the Christian God cannot just happen to be a fiction, a product of human thought, imagination etc. Rather, if there is no such God, if he is a fiction, then there can be no such God: he is necessarily a fiction, for, like the square circle, he is impossible. One of the traditional objections to the argument, therefore, that it consists in an illegitimate move from thought to reality, may more clearly be seen to be mistaken. For the argument points out that there is something of which it is true that it is either an impossible fiction (a logically incoherent thought) or a real, non-fictional entity, since the possibility that it be a possible fiction (a logically coherent thought, but one which happens to be uninstantiated) is excluded. For suppose that x is a possible fiction; then it cannot be a necessary existent, since, precisely because it is a fiction, it is logically possible that it should not have been conceived, and thus that it should not exist, for the existence of fictions is contingent upon their being conceived. But God is a necessary existent: therefore he cannot be a possible fiction. Thus, either he is a real entity, or an impossible fiction. Either there is a God, or 'God' is incoherent. Just as the square circle is necessarily both square and circular, and therefore an impossible fiction, so God necessarily exists, and is therefore either an impossible fiction or a necessarily instantiated non-fiction. Rather than being a movement from thought to reality, then, the ontological argument consists in an analysis of a particular idea, to show what must be the nature of the entity which is its instantiation; and Anselm's failure is a failure to consider the alternative possibility to the one he describes. God may be defined as that which is the most real possible, but nevertheless be a fiction: for if the definition turns out to be incoherent, then God is necessarily a fiction, since what is defined is an impossible entity, and all impossible entities are fictions.

Anselm fails to consider this possibility because it does not occur to him that a Fool might argue that 'God' is a nonsense, that the definition with which he begins — 'God is that than which nothing greater can be thought' — is one which is incoherent. This flaw is thus present right from the start, in ch. II, and not in ch. III: for Anselm, having established that God exists in ch. II, could go on from (7) above to show that God necessarily exists, since, given that God exists, it is most certainly possible that he exists. The point is of course that it is ch. II in which the argument itself is to be found, and that it is an argument which does not rely for its formal consistency on the idea of necessary existence. If necessary existence were no part of 'the most real entity possible', then the argument in ch. II would remain unaffected: it is simply that the business of inquiring into the sense of 'the most real entity possible' would take a different form. But in that case of course God would not be at all the sort of being which Christianity takes him to be. Were it not the case that 'something can be thought to exist that cannot be thought not to exist, and this is greater than that which can be thought not to exist' (*Pros.* III, p. 119) and God were alleged to be merely contingently real, then the problem would immediately arise as to the difference between God and items in the world (his creation). To insist on God's eternity and aseity, and with that on his logically necessary existence, is to differentiate between God and everything else, or at least between God and all empirical, or material, entities: the most bounteous island, the most perfect saint, the sum of all the thalers ever minted, even the universe itself, are all excluded as candidates for the definition, 'the most real entity possible'. If the notion of necessary existence is incoherent, and it cannot be a necessary condition of something's being the most real entity possible that its existence be necessary, then on what grounds could a particular entity be picked out as being the most real possible? All contingent entities are to some extent alike in respect of their reality, precisely because they are contingent: it is necessary existence that marks off God from his creation.

Anselm does not address the question of the intelligibility and coherence of 'that than which nothing greater can be thought', that is, of the idea of an eternal and self-sufficient, and thus necessarily existent being. That this is so has on the one hand served to obscure the argument of *Proslogion* II; and on the other explains certain exegetical difficulties. The centrality of this for a proper understanding of the argument may become clearer by considering the basis on which Anselm proposes his definition. To echo another question, does Anselm hold God to be maximally real because eternal and self-sufficient, or are timelessness and self-sufficiency the conditions of maximal reality because God is eternal and self-sufficient? Does Anselm begin with platonic metaphysics, into which he is able to fit God as that which is maximally real because he thinks that it is God, who, being eternal and self-sufficient, measures up to the standard of maximal reality laid down by the metaphysical system? Or does he rather choose this particular system because he thinks it an accurate account of how things are inasmuch as its standard of maximal reality coincides with certain of God's features? The question is of course intended as a logical, and not a psychological, one. It is tempting to suppose that it is the Christian conception of God which logically precedes Greek metaphysics in Anselm's thought, and this is certainly a view which would reinforce the criticism that his argument is trivially circular. Consider the following from the *Proslogion*:

> But clearly, whatever You are, You are not that through another but through Your very self. You are therefore the very life by which You live, the wisdom by which You are wise, the very goodness by which You are good to both good men and wicked, and the same holds for like attributes.   — ch. XII, p. 133

Now this passage might suggest that since God has his life, wisdom, and goodness 'through [His] very self', it is his being God which renders his being and his attributes supreme. And if this notion is applied to the assertion that God is 'the being who [alone] exists in a strict and absolute sense' (*Pros.* XXII, p. 145) ('You are...the very life by which You live...') we find that God is maximally real simply inasmuch as he is God: 'If God is God, God exists. And since the antecedent is evident, the conclusion is evident likewise.'[54] However, the antecedent, 'God is God' is crucially ambiguous. Were this view of Anselm's grounds for saying that God is maximally real an accurate interpretation of his thought, then 'God' would in both its instances function as a proper name. But since definitions cannot be given of proper names or their bearers, Anselm's formula would have to be treated as a description, and not a definition, of God, with the result that Anselm could not show that the Fool contradicts himself if he accepts the formula but not the conclusion. Anselm would be saying merely that God, since he is to be described as maximally real, is real: God, being God, exists. The argument would indeed be trivially circular, and hardly an argument at all. If the formula is taken as a definition of God, however, and I have argued in ch. 3 that the balance of evidence favours such an interpretation, then it must be a definition of whatever it is which is God, that is, of 'God' as a descriptive predicable. Bonaventure's view will therefore have to be understood like this: God (= proper name) is God (= descriptive predicable); therefore he exists. This would in turn suggest that God is maximally real because he has the features required for an entity to be maximally real, and that these are logically independent of God, their bearer.

In what follows, then, I shall use 'God' when using the word as a proper name, and 'god' when using it as a descriptive predicable, except in those instances where I quote, whether directly or indirectly, and do not wish to introduce a distinction which the author does not make. In such cases I shall use 'God'.[55]

Once the distinction between 'God' and 'god' is recognized, it is clear that it must be God's being god which makes his being and his attributes supreme. Anselm derives his idea of ontological supremacy, not from God's traditional attributes, but from Greek metaphysics: at least, this is how the logic of his thought moves, whatever its psychological movement. He regards God as maximally real because he measures up to logically independent standards of reality. This seems in fact quite clear from the body of the thoroughly platonic *Monologion* text, and is strongly suggested by other passages from the *Proslogion*. In ch. XIII for example, we read:

> All that which is enclosed in any way by place or time is less than that which no law of place or time constrains. Since, then, nothing is greater than You, no place or time confines You but You exist everywhere and always. — p. 133

God, being supremely great, must be unconfined by place or time because so to be unconfined is a condition of maximal greatness: the argument moves from the metaphysical principle to the definition of God, and so to his being unlimited. Perhaps the clearest passage in the *Proslogion* to support this view is in ch. XXII:

> And You are the being who exists in a strict and absolute sense because You have neither past nor future existence but only present existence; nor can You be thought not to exist at any time. — p. 145

Necessarily existing only in the present (which is for Anselm synonymous with existing 'neither yesterday nor today nor tomorrow but [being] absolutely outside all time' (*Pros.* XIX, p. 141)) is a condition of existence 'in a strict and absolute sense'. This follows the pattern of argument of the *Proslogion* as a whole: God is defined as that which is supremely real, from which it is deduced that God cannot be a fiction, and that he is moreover eternal, self-sufficient, etc.

In terms of *Proslogion* II — IV then, we may say that Anselm does not distinguish between 'deus' as a description of 'dominus', and 'deus' as the name of him who is 'dominus'. Thus in ch. II he addresses 'domine' (*God*) as 'You who give understanding to faith', saying of him (*god*) that he is 'something than which nothing greater can be thought'. In ch. III he addresses God as 'domine deus noster/meus' (*god*): 'And You [*God*], Lord our God [*god*], are this being' (which cannot be thought not to exist). In ch. IV, 'God [*god*], is that than which nothing greater can be thought'. In the *Reply* of course, where Gaunilo, and not God, is addressed, his usage is much more consistent with that in *Proslogion* IV.

Furthermore, if the distinction between *God* and *god* is applied to certain passages in Anselm which are puzzling when considered against the interpretation of the text which I am proposing, the puzzlement is fairly readily removed. Firstly, the very introduction in ch. II of Anselm's formula:

> Now we believe that You are something than which nothing greater can be thought. — p. 117

I have argued that this must be taken as a definition in order to carry the Fool along at all; but if it is so taken, then what it defines cannot be a proper name or its bearer. And yet it is quite clear that Anselm is addressing God, and just as clear that simply to state that 'we believe' that God is something than which nothing greater can be thought is hardly an adequate starting-point for his argument. The Fool knows very well that Anselm and his fellow believers believe it — but he does not. What Anselm and the Fool do believe in common, since they share a common metaphysics, is that *god* is something than which nothing greater can be thought. And they both believe it because it is for both of them a matter of definition. Anselm is able to have it both ways because he does not distinguish *God* from *god*. Now consider again the first paragraph of Anselm's *Reply*:

> I reply as follows: If 'that than which a greater cannot be thought' is neither understood nor thought of, and is neither in the mind nor in thought, then it is evident that *either* God is not that than which a greater cannot be thought *or* is not understood nor thought of, and is not in the mind nor in thought. Now my strongest argument that this is false is to appeal to your faith and to your conscience. — *Reply* I, p. 169

Here it is clear that Anselm is not appealing, as he was when addressing the Fool, to a belief shared in virtue of a metaphysics shared, but rather to a belief shared in virtue of a religious faith shared. This is of course what he sets out in his *Reply* to do: 'Since it is not the Fool, against whom I spoke in my tract, who takes me up, but one who, though speaking on the Fool's behalf, is an orthodox Christian and no fool, it will suffice if I reply to the Christian.' (Preface, p. 169). But if Anselm is replying to the Christian alone, he cannot seriously be taking Gaunilo to be speaking on the Fool's behalf. Anselm uses *'God'* as a proper name here, and appeals to Gaunilo's faith and conscience that the bearer of the name is indeed *god*, i.e., that than which nothing greater can be thought. This alone would be in order — Anselm may appeal to a Christian's faith and conscience on matters of Christian belief. Nor would there be anything objectionable to such an appeal to agree also that God is understood and thought of if it were directed against the Thomistic kind of objection that God cannot (essentially) be known — but it is not so directed. It is directed against the objection that 'that than which nothing greater can be thought' cannot be understood, that is, against an objection to a metaphysical tenet, the tenet that 'that which is maximally real', i.e. *'god'*, is unintelligible: for Anselm continues, 'Therefore "that than which a greater cannot be thought" is truly understood and thought and is in the mind and in thought.' (p. 169) And in such a case an appeal to faith and conscience is misdirected. However, if it is borne in mind that Anselm does not distinguish *God* from *god*, the confusion here becomes clearly explicable precisely as stemming from the failure to make such a distinction.

Finally, I shall consider the conclusion of *Reply* X, where it would perhaps appear that Anselm does make a distinction very much like the one which I maintain is absent from his thought:

> I think now that I have shown that I have proved in the above tract, not by a weak argumentation but by a sufficiently necessary one, that something than which a greater cannot be thought exists in reality itself, and that this proof has not been weakened by the force of any objection. For the import of this proof is in itself of such force that what is spoken of is proved (as a necessary consequence of the fact that it is understood or thought of) both to exist in actual reality and to be itself whatever must be believed about the Divine Being. For we believe of the Divine Being whatever it can, absolutely speaking, be thought better to be than not to be. For example, it is better to be eternal than not eternal, good than not good, indeed goodness-itself than not goodness-itself. However, nothing of this kind cannot but be that than which a greater cannot be thought. It is, then, necessary that 'that than which a greater cannot be thought' should be whatever must be believed about the Divine Nature.
>
> — pp. 189—191

From the first two sentences, it seems that Anselm is saying that he has proved that that which is *god* ('something than which a greater cannot be thought') is real, and has those attributes and that nature which we (namely Christians) must believe *God* to have. For we believe, he continues, that *God* is eternal, and that he is good; but anything which is these must be that which is maximally real, i.e., that which is *god* ('that than which a greater cannot be thought'). That which is *god*, therefore, must have those attributes we believe *God* to have and thus be what *God* is. Anselm might be thought to be distinguishing in the last sentence that than which nothing greater can be thought from the Divine Nature, and to conclude that he has succeeded in doing what he set out in ch. II of the *Proslogion* to do, namely to understand that 'You exist as we believe You to exist, and that You are what we believe You to be' by showing that the being here referred to, *God*, is indeed that than which nothing greater can be thought, i.e. *god*. One may gain from this the impression, as La Croix has, that Anselm's whole purpose in the *Proslogion* is to prove that whatever it is which is such that nothing greater can be thought is real, and that it is of such and such a kind; and then, on grounds of 'faith and conscience' to identify this entity with the bearer of the name God. This would of course entail that Anselm's formula be taken as a description and not a definition. But then, as I have argued, the Fool would hardly need convincing, given that he shares Anselm's metaphysics; and he would certainly not be impressed by the assertion of a certain description of the Divine Being ('For we believe of the Divine Being whatever it can, absolutely speaking, be thought better to be than not to be.' (*Reply* X, p. 191)) on the basis of which Anselm states his conclusion. It is of course the case that Anselm does fail to establish the identification of *God*, rather than some other entity, as *god*. But surely there can be no question that it is Anselm's intention to convince the Fool, and that, had he the distinction clearly in mind between *God* and *god*, between the Divine Being and that than which a greater cannot be thought, he would have realized that — given the distinction — he could not convince the Fool that he is contradicting himself in asserting that there is no *God*, but that the contradiction would arise only if the Fool were to deny that there is that than which nothing greater can be thought, i.e. *god*.

Far more likely is that because Anselm simply does not make the distinction, the apparent naivety of the passage is as real as it is apparent. Certainly, chs. V — XXV of the *Proslogion* constitute an argument that God is as 'we believe You to be', i.e., that having the divine attributes follows from God's being that than which nothing greater can be thought: and clearly, this is effectively an argument that it is *God* who is to be identified as *god*. That than which nothing greater can be thought, namely *god*, must be something with such-and-such attributes, since to have these follows from being maximally real; these attributes are just those which are traditionally ascribed to the entity named *God*; therefore it is *God* who is *god*.

Nevertheless, although Anselm's argument is in effect as just outlined, this clearly does not represent his intention. Rather, his intention in these chapters is to show that God, who is that than which nothing greater can be thought, must have just those attributes which tradition ascribes to him, since it follows from the definition that the entity so defined should have them. Part of what he is doing is to attempt to explain how someone like God can be said to have those attributes, how they are to be understood (e.g. ch. VI, 'How He is perceptive although He is not a body'). There is, however, no question at all — for Anselm — of having to succeed in doing that in order to justify the definition he gives in ch. II. That the attributes follow from the definition is for Anselm confirmation that God indeed has them, that 'You are as we believe You to be'; and that they are so deducible is what he expects to convince the Fool that this is so, rather than being something he intends to function as a justification for identifying that than which nothing greater can be thought as God. He does not see that the intelligibility of the definition with which he starts is in fact dependent on the very possibility of its being given some specific content. For him, a suggestion such as Geach's that 'the proposition "A God exists"...affirms that something-or-other has Divine attributes'[56] is to put matters back to front. Rather, 'God exists' affirms that he who has divine attributes exists. Thus the *possibility* of something's having divine attributes is not for him at issue: nor is there any question of having to show that it is *God* who has the attributes of that than which nothing greater can be thought.

Chapter 6

Conclusion

The question of whether God, the personal being of the Judaeo-Christian tradition, *can* have the attributes of eternity and self-sufficiency, is its fundamental problem. There is no more powerful statement of the dilemma than Feuerbach's:

> The grand principle, the central point of Christian sophistry, is the idea of God. God is the human being, and yet he must be regarded as another, a superhuman being. God is universal, abstract being, simply the idea of being; and yet he must be conceived as personal, individual being; — or God is a person, and yet he must be regarded as God, as universal, i.e., not as a personal being. God is; his existence is certain, more certain than ours; he has an existence distinct from us and from things in general, i.e., an individual existence; and yet his existence must be held a spiritual one, i.e., an existence not perceptible as a special one ...A God who does not trouble himself about us, who does not hear our prayers, who does not see and love us, is no God; thus humanity is made an essential predicate of God; — but at the same time it is said: A God who does not exist in and by himself, out of men, above men, as another being, is a phantom; and thus it is made an essential predicate of God that he is non-human and extra-human. A God who is not as we are, who has not consciousness, not intelligence, i.e., not a personal understanding, a personal consciousness (as, for example, the 'substance' of Spinoza), is no God. Essential identity with us is the chief condition of deity; the idea of deity is made dependent on the idea of personality, of consciousness, *quo nihil majus cogitari potest*. But it is said in the same breath, a God who is not essentially distinguished from us is no God.[1]

As I have argued earlier, no general fiat issued against the possibility of any necessarily existent entity will do, for the assumptions governing it are just those that the proponent denies. Christians must deny, for example, that 'Fictional or purely ideational conceptualizations apart, there is only one sort or level of existence and this is to have a place in space-time.'[2] What is required to resolve this issue, perhaps *the* metaphysical issue, is an investigation of the particular case, to determine whether or not the candidate proposed for the office and title of necessary existent could be the sort of entity which could logically occupy it. The problem, then, is this. A necessary being must be eternal and self-sufficient: but is it conceivable that God, given the qualities and attributes he is held to have, should be such an entity? Is it logically possible that an eternal and self-sufficient being should, for example, act in the world? Or to put the same question in the terms I introduced at the end of the last chapter: can *God*, the personal being of the Judaeo-Christian tradition, be *god*, the necessarily existent metaphysical absolute inherited from the Greeks?

Anselm's argument, in accurately reflecting this internal tension in the 'God' of Christianity, exemplifies the problems surrounding the concept of the being whose existence it sets out to prove. This is its central, albeit inadvertent, achievement: in demonstrating how and why the question of the existence of the God of Christianity is a *logical* question, it points up what is peculiarly problematic about it. *In fine* it shows how it is that the question of the existence of God is one and the same as the question of the intelligibility and coherence of 'God': to ask whether God exists is to ask whether it is possible to talk coherently of God; and in discussing the possibility of such talk, one is discussing the possibility of the existence of God. For if it is possible that God both is eternal and self-sufficient and has the personal attributes, or some of them, traditionally ascribed to him, then it is possible that 'God exists' is necessarily true; and if 'God exists' could be necessarily true, then it *is* necessarily true. Alternatively, if it cannot be shown how the difficulties in ascribing any such attributes to an eternal and self-sufficient entity may be overcome — if, that is, no satisfactory account of God-talk is available — then all that is left is something which is eternally and self-sufficiently whatever it is, if anything at all. And this is no more than an empty absolute, the emptiness of which would weigh conclusively against acceptance of the metaphysical system whose culmination it was. Finally, if it were shown conclusively that such difficulties cannot be overcome, then it would have been shown that 'God exists' is necessarily false: the God of Christianity could not possibly exist. Whether these difficulties are *prima facie* ones which we have not yet found the means to overcome, or whether they are ones of a kind which in priciple cannot be overcome, is not my task to settle here. It is enough that Anselm's argument should raise the question.

Notes

Introduction

1 An excellent review of the history of the argument is to be found in Charles Hartshorne, *Anselm's Discovery* (Open Court, La Salle, Ill. 1965), and a shorter one in *St. Anselm's 'Proslogion' with 'A Reply on Behalf of the Fool' by Gaunilo and 'The Author's Reply to Gaunilo'*, translated with an introduction and philosophical commentary by M. J. Charlesworth (Oxford University Press 1965). Both also deal with the relation of Descartes' argument to that of Anselm: I argue that the former is inferior in 'Pure Objects and the Ontological Argument', *Sophia*, XIV (1975) pp. 10-18. The definitive medieval history is A. Daniels' collection of C13th. texts referring to the *Proslogion*: 'Quellenbeiträge und Untersuchungen zur Geschichte der Gottesbeweise im XIII Jahrhundert', in *Beiträge zur Geschichte der Philosophie des Mittelalters*, 8, 1-2 (Aschendorffsche Verlagsbuchhandlung, Münster 1909). For details of Anselm's life, see ed. R. W. Southern, *Eadmer, 'The Life of Anselm'* (Nelson, London 1962); R. W. Southern, *St Anselm and his Biographer* (Cambridge University Press 1963); and ed. R. W. Southern and F. S. Schmitt, *Memorials of St. Anselm* (Oxford University Press 1969).

2 *From Belief to Understanding* (Australian National University, Canberra 1976).

3 *Proslogion II and III* (E. J. Brill, Leiden 1972).

4 Karl Barth, *Anselm: Fides Quaerens Intellectum* (SCM, London 1960). Cf. Anselm Stolz, 'Zur Theologie Anselms im Proslogion', *Catholica*, 2, 1933, pp. 1-24 (translated in ed. John Hick and Arthur McGill, *The Many-Faced Argument* (Macmillan, London 1968), pp. 183-206); and André Hayen, 'St. Anselme et St. Thomas. La vraie nature de la théologie et sa portée apostolique', in *Spicilegium Beccense* (J. Vrin, Paris 1959), pp. 45-85 (the second part translated as 'The Role of the Fool in St. Anselm and the Necessarily Apostolic Character of True Christian Reflection', in ed. John Hick and Arthur McGill, op. cit., pp. 162-182).

5 Cf. Paul J. W. Miller, 'The Ontological Argument for God', *The Personalist*, 42 (1961), pp. 337-351, and Sylvia Fleming Crocker, 'The

Ontological Significance of Anselm's *Proslogion*', *The Modern Schoolman*, 50 (1972), pp. 33-56.
6 Bonaventure, *De Myst. Trin.* I, 1, 29; cited by Etienne Gilson, *The Philosophy of Bonaventure*, trans. by Dom Illtyd Trethowan and F. J. Sheed (Sheed and Ward, London 1940), p. 128.
7 Schiller, *Wallenstein-Trilogie: Piccolomini*, Act ii, sc. 7; quoted by Arthur Schopenhauer in *The Fourfold Root of the Principle of Sufficient Reason*, given in ed. Alvin Plantinga, *The Ontological Argument* (Macmillan, London 1968), p. 67.

Chapter 1

1 Richard Campbell, for example, says that Anselm uses these words 'apparently interchangeably': *From Belief to Understanding* (Australian National University, Canberra 1976), pp. 72 and 133. This leads him to miss the centrality of the metaphysics within which Anselm is operating, and thus to underestimate the role of the Fool. As a result he offers an interpretation of the argument which seriously underplays its *philosophical* importance.
2 *St. Anselm's 'Proslogion'...* (Oxford Univesity Press 1965), p. 64.
3 'Anselm's Ontological Arguments', in ed. John Hick and Arthur McGill, *The Many-Faced Argument* (Macmillan, London 1968), p. 303.
4 See ch. 3, p. 59 ff.
5 *Monologion*, Preface, p. 36.
6 *Scholastik*, 9 (1934), pp. 400-409.
7 ibid., p. 403, my translation. For detailed citation of Augustine see Stolz's article.
8 ibid., p. 404.
9 *City of God*, VIII, 11; cited by Stolz, op. cit., p. 404.
10 ibid., pp. 406-7.
11 Charlesworth, op. cit.
12 'Degress of Reality in Plato', in ed. Renford Bambrough, *New Essays on Plato and Aristotle* (RKP, London 1965), pp. 1-20.
13 Paul J. W. Miller, 'The Ontological Argument for God', *The Personalist*, 42 (1961), p. 348.
14 *Monologion*, III, p. 42. See also ch. XXVIII, and *Proslogion* XXII.
15 *Republic*, 508e-509.
16 Cf. *Proslogion* XXII, XXIII, and *Monologion*, I, IV.
17 Para. 6 of Gaunilo's *Reply on Behalf of the Fool*, p. 165, from which the following quotations are taken.
18 *The Philosophical Works of Descartes*, trans. by E. S. Haldane and G. R. T. Ross (Cambridge University Press, 1970), vol. II, p. 187.
19 ibid., p. 8.
20 *The Fourfold Root of the Principle of Sufficient Reason*, in ed. Alvin Plantinga, *The Ontological Argument* (Macmillan, London 1968), pp. 65-67.
21 *The Rise of Scientific Philosophy* (University of California, Berkeley 1951), p. 39.
22 *The Ontological Argument* (Macmillan, London 1972), p. 28.

23 *De Myst. Trin.* Q. 1, a. 1, sol. opp. 6, given by A. Daniels, 'Quellenbeiträge und Untersuchungen zur Geschichte der Gottesbeweise im XIII Jahrhundert', in *Beiträge zur Geschichte der Philosophie des Mittelalters*, 8, 1-2 (Aschendorffsche Verlagsbuchhandlung, Münster 1909), p. 40; cited by Hick and McGill, op. cit., p. 24, fn. 12.
24 'The Ontological Disproof of the Devil', *Analysis*, 17 (1957), pp. 71-2.
25 'The Ontological Proof of the Devil', *Philosophical Studies*, 9 (1958), pp. 63-4. I think this red herring was first floated by Albert A. Cock in 'The Ontological Argument for the Existence of God', *PAS*, 18 (1918), pp. 363-384. The rather amusing debate arising from Richman's article, and which depends upon a resolute refusal to distinguish 'maius' from 'melius', may be traced through the following: Theodore Waldman, 'A Comment Upon the Ontological Proof of the Devil', *Philosophical Studies*, 10 (1959), pp. 59-60; Robert J. Richman, 'The Devil and Dr. Waldman', *Philosophical Studies*, 11 (1960), pp. 78-80; Oliver A. Johnson, 'God and St. Anselm', *Journal of Religion*, 45 (1965), pp. 326-334; David and Marjorie Haight, 'An Ontological Argument for the Devil', *The Monist*, 54 (1970), pp. 218-220; Wolfgang L. F. Gombocz, 'St. Anselm's Disproof of the Devil's Existence. A Counter Argument Against Haight and Richman', *Ratio*, 15 (1973), pp. 334-337; Robert J. Richman, 'A Serious Look at the Ontological Argument', *Ratio*, 18 (1976), pp. 85-89; Wolfgang L. Gombocz, 'St. Anselm's Two Devils But One God', *Ratio*, 20 (1978), pp. 142-146 (in which he claims without argument that whether Anselm is using 'maius' or 'melius' 'doesn't make the slightest difference' — p. 143!); W. J. Wainright, 'On an Alleged Incoherence in Anselm's Argument: A Reply to Robert Richman', ibid., pp. 147-148; and Wlodzimierz Rabinowicz, 'An Alleged New Refutation of St. Anselm's Argument', ibid., pp. 149-150.

Chapter 2

1 See also e.g., *Cur Deus Homo*, I, VI, p. 186; II, VII, p. 246; II, X, pp. 252, 254; and *Monologion*, LXXIX, p. 143.
2 See also e.g., *Cur Deus Homo*, I, X, pp. 200-1; I, XVIII, p. 216; II, VIII, p. 248; II, XVI, p. 267: and *Monologion*, LXXIV, p. 139.
3 *The Logic of St. Anselm* (Oxford University Press, 1967), p. 178.
4 D. P. Henry's term: Charlesworth's is 'syllogistic necessity'.
5 See also e.g., *Monologion*, I, pp. 38-40; II, p. 40; IV, p. 43; VII, p. 51; XIII, p. 60; XIX, p. 70; XXIX, p. 90; XXXI, p. 92; XXXV, p. 99; XXXVIII, p. 101; XLI, p. 104; LI, p. 115; LIII, p. 115; LVII, p. 119; LXV, p. 131; LXXII, p. 138; LXXVIII, p. 143: and *Cur Deus Homo*, I, X, p. 201; I, XXV, p. 237; II, IX, p. 251.
6 Interestingly, perhaps, 'Moreover, there is one thing needful' in the Authorized Version.
7 'The Irreducibly Modal Structure of the Argument', in ed. John Hick and Arthur McGill, *The Many-Faced Argument* (Macmillan, London 1968), p. 335 (ch. 2, sec. VI of *The Logic of Perfection* (Open

Court, La Salle, Ill. 1962)). Cf. Norman Malcolm, 'Anselm's Ontological Arguments', ibid., pp. 301-320.
8 D. P. Henry, *Medieval Logic and Metaphysics* (Hutchinson, London 1972), pp. 108-9.
9 ibid., p. 108.
10 See also e.g., *Reply* II, p. 173; V, p. 183; IX, p. 189; X, p. 189: and Gaunilo's *Reply* I, p. 157; 5, p. 163; 7, p. 165.Hartshorne brackets chs. V and IX of Anselm's *Reply* with ch. I in arguing for his reinterpretation; and this leads one to suspect that Anselm's 'inferential necessity' plays an important part in misleading him.
11 Charlesworth omits 'to exist' from his translation, although it appears in Anselm's Latin: 'si vel cogitari potest esse...' (p. 168). This omission could be misleading, since Anselm is trying to show that if God can be thought to exist, then he exists; and not that if God can be conceived at all, then he exists. He argues the latter later on in *Reply* I.
12 Charles Hartshorne, *Anselm's Discovery* (Open Court, La Salle, Ill. 1965), pp. 15, 34, 87, 93.
13 This premiss is not stated explicitly in the *Proslogion* or *Reply*: but see *Proslogion* XIX and XX, and *Monologion* XVIII.
14 *Dialogue on Truth*, in *Selections from Medieval Philosophers*, ed. and trans. by Richard McKeon (Charles Scribner's Sons, N.Y. 1929): '...nothing is true except by participating in truth, and therefore the truth of what is true is in that which is true; but the thing stated is not in the true statement and therefore it must be called, not the truth of it, but the cause of its truth' (p. 153).
15 Introduction to S. N. Deane, *St. Anselm: Basic Writings* (Open Court, La Salle, Ill. 1962, 2nd ed.), p. 3.
16 Cf. *Reply* I, p. 173. This is of course in accord with Anselm's epistemology in his *Dialogue on Truth*.
17 This makes it the more odd that Henry should think that the sense of 'greater than' in ch. III is 'quite diverse from that which figures in the Chapter 2 proof' (*The Logic of St. Anselm*, op. cit., p. 146). But see also Richard Campbell, *From Belief to Understanding* (Australian National University, Canberra 1976), ch. 6, for a different emphasis.
18 ed. Hick and McGill, op. cit., p. 26, fn. 14.
19 But see the quotation from *Reply* III, on p. 30, and fn. 16.
20 For a critique of Hartshorne's modal argument *per se*, see my 'Hartshorne's Modal Argument for the Existence of God', *Ratio*, 17 (1976), pp. 140-146.

Chapter 3

1 But cf. Richard Campbell, *From Belief to Understanding* (Australian National University, Canberra 1976), p. 31ff., whose attribution to Anselm of the deliberate use of (a)/(c) and (b)/(d) as indefinite and definite descriptions respectively is a function of his semifideistic interpretation of the argument. See also Jasper Hopkins, 'On Understanding and Preunderstanding St. Anselm', *New Scholasticism*, 52 (1978), p. 254 fn. 13.

2 *Anselm: Fides Quaerens Intellectum* (SCM, London 1960), pp. 73-89.
3 Richard R. La Croix, *Proslogion II and III* (E. J. Brill, Leiden 1972), pp. 14-19.
4 op. cit., p. 20ff.
5 See my review of *Proslogion II and III* in *Philosophical Studies* (Eire), XXIII (1975), pp. 314-317.
6 op. cit., p. 27. Campbell's interpretation, although interesting and often perspicuous, is finally unconvincing, in respect both of philosophical interpretation of Anselm, and of some of the points of translation central to his thesis. The definitive critique is Jasper Hopkins 'On Understanding and Preunderstanding St. Anselm', op. cit., pp. 243-260.
7 ibid. Cf. p. 43, fn. 13 of the present text.
8 See Jasper Hopkins, op. cit., p. 254, fn. 14: 'It is noteworthy that in what appears to be an *early* draft of the *Proslogion* Anselm wrote (in the section which corresponds to Chapter 2): "Similiter insipiens homo convincitur esse vel in intellectu aliquid, quo nihil maius cogitari potest, *scilicet deum*, quia cum audit hoc dici intelligit aliquo modo...".' This would seem to dispose to Campbell's view that *Proslogion* III and IV are arguments for the indentification of God with that than which nothing greater can be thought, rather than a drawing out of certain characteristics of the God who has been shown in *Proslogion* II to exist on the basis of what is said of him in that proof. Cf. Hopkins' discussion of the opening prayer of *Proslogion* II, ibid., pp. 249-50.
9 op. cit., p. 26.
10 La Croix's objections against allowing 'is possible' as a synonym for Anselm's 'can be thought', which he argues is permissible 'only if we are willing to allow that in Chapter XV Anselm intended either to assert that God is logically impossible or to put forward a meaningless statement' (op. cit., p. 51) are similarly invalid; as is also Gareth Matthews' argument in 'On Conceivability in Anselm and Aquinas', *Philosophical Review*, 70 (1961), pp. 110-11.
11 op. cit., p. 205.
12 Cf. Jasper Hopkins, *A Companion to the Study of St. Anselm* (University of Minnesota Press, Minneapolis 1972), pp. 74-6.
13 Campbell's citing of *Reply* I as evidence in favour of his thesis that Anselm is concerned in *Proslogion* II with proving the existence of that than which nothing greater can be thought rather than that of God neglects this central point.
14 *A Companion to the Study of St. Anselm*, op. cit., p. 40.
15 See Anselm's *Dialogue on Truth*, in ed. and trans. by Richard McKeon, *Selections from Medieval Philosophers* (Charles Scribner's Sons, N.Y. 1929), vol. I, pp. 150-184; and Campbell's excellent discussion of it in 'Anselm's Background Metaphysics', *Scottish Journal of Theology*, 33 (1980), pp. 317-343.
16 *Anselm: Fides Quaerens Intellectum*, op. cit., p. 165.
17 'Even in respect of the most obstinate unbeliever it can be accomplished that the inner consistency and to that extent the meaning of the Gospel-message is intelligible to him.' — *Church Dogmatics* (T. & T. Clark,

Edinburgh 1936 onwards), IV, 3, p. 848. Barth appears to be arguing that terms can be known to be consistent or inconsistent even though they are not properly understood, a quite remarkably odd view.

18 Cf. Charlesworth, *St. Anselm's 'Proslogion'*... (Oxford University Press, 1965), pp. 27-8.

19 *Anselm: Fides Quaerens Intellectum*, op. cit., pp. 99-100.

20 ibid., p. 100.

21 See e.g., *Church Dogmatics*, op. cit., I, 1, p. 148n.: 'For we know nothing of our created state, but only through the Word of God...To "start from man" can only mean to start with man of the lost *status integritatis*, that is, of the presently existing *status corruptionis*...There is a way from Christology to anthropology. There is no way from anthropology to Christology.'

22 'After I had published, at the pressing entreaties of several of my brethren, a certain short tract [the *Monologion*] as an example of meditation on the meaning of faith from the point of view of one seeking, through silent reasoning within himself, things he knows not — reflecting that this was made up of a connected chain of many arguments...'. — *Proslogion*, Preface, p. 103.

23 McKeon himself claims in his introduction that 'It is important [for Anselm] that faith precede understanding, since of the two sources of human knowledge, reason and faith , faith can exist without reason, but reason can not exist without faith. In rational inquiry there must be a foundation of faith in the principles of the inquiry and in the principles of the understanding itself.' (op. cit., p. 142; quoted by Charlesworth, op. cit., p. 37, fn. 1). There is a confusion here between religious faith and faith in reason. The former plays no part in the *Dialogue*, whereas the latter is just what makes Anselm's writing philosophical, and not purely theological.

24 *Review of Metaphysics*, 27 (1974), pp. 513-530. Cosgrove offers a comprehensive discussion of all Aquinas's objections, showing that they are either to be subsumed under that in *Summa Contra Gentiles*, I, 11, or fail to strike against Anselm's argument.

25 'Aquinas On Saying That God Doesn't Exist', *The Monist*, 47 (1963), pp. 472-477; cited by Cosgrove as the basis of his own interpretation.

26 *Summa Theologica*, Ia, q. 2, a. 1. ad. 1.

27 Cf. *In Primum Librum Sententiarum*, dist. 3, q. 1, a. 2, 4 (also cited by Cosgrove, op. cit., p. 523): '...the reasoning of Anselm is to be understood thus. After we understand God, it is not possible that it be understood that God exists, and that he could be thought not to exist; but from this it does not follow that someone could not deny or think that God does not exist; for he can think that nothing of this sort exists than which a greater cannot be thought; and therefore his reasoning proceeds from this supposition, that it should be supposed that something does exist than which a greater cannot be thought.' Cosgrove thinks that this is the same objection, since, if Aquinas were making a factual, and not a logical, claim about that than which a greater cannot be thought, he would be begging the question against Anselm, as in his reply in the *Summa Theologica* (Ia, q. 2, a. 1, ad. 2), where Anselm's

argument is simply ignored. In fact, it seems to me that this is a quite different objection, directed against the argument of *Proslogion* III, which Aquinas does not misinterpret as a modal argument for the existence of God. Having correctly summarized Anselm's argument ('God is that than which a greater cannot be thought. But that which cannot be thought not to exist is greater than that which can be thought not to exist. Therefore God cannot be thought not to exist, since he is that than which nothing greater can be thought.' (dist. 3, q. 1, a. 2, 4)) he objects to Anselm's claim that God cannot be thought not to exist, since it is based on the conclusion of *Proslogion* II, a conclusion which Aquinas does not accept. Anselm's reasoning does indeed proceed from the supposition that 'something exists than which a greater cannot be thought'; but Aquinas's objection here assumes the success of his argument against *Proslogion* II.

28 Charles Hartshorne, *Anselm's Discovery* (Open Court, La Salle, Ill., 1965), p. 161.
29 Cosgrove, op. cit., p. 527.
30 *Summa Contra Gentiles*, I, 11.
31 op. cit., p. 475.
32 ibid., p. 473.
33 ibid., p. 475.
34 See Jonathan Barnes, *The Ontological Argument* (Macmillan, London 1972), p. 10.
35 Charlesworth, op. cit., p. 64.
36 ibid., p. 68.
37 'The Ontological Argument for God', *The Personalist*, 42 (1961), p. 346.
38 Hutchinson, London 1972, pp. 116-7.
39 Cornell University Press, Ithaca 1967.
40 ibid., pp. 67-71.
41 ibid., p. 72.
42 ibid., p. 74.
43 ibid.
44 ibid.
45 ibid.
46 ibid.
47 ibid., p. 76.
48 ibid. Plantinga's argument continues: 'hence it is false that there is no Guatemalan greater than Hector. Our proof, however, depended upon no special facts about Hector; hence we can generalize our conclusion to the result that for any Guatemalan there is a greater. Given that the relation *greater than* is transitive, irreflexive, and asymmetrical, it follows that the set of Guatemalans is infinite. Hence if there are any Guatemalans at all, there is an infinite set of them.'
49 ibid., p. 80.
50 ibid.
51 ibid., p. 72.
52 Schopenhauer, *The Fourfold Root of the Principle of Sufficient Reason*, trans. by K. Hillebrand (George Bell & Sons, London 1897, rev. ed.): given in ed. A. Plantinga, *The Ontological Argument* (Macmillan, London 1968), ch. 7, p. 66.

53 ibid., p. 67.
54 *New Essays Concerning Human Understanding*, trans. by A. G. Langley (Open Court, La Salle, Ill. 1949, 3rd. ed.): given in A. Plantinga, op. cit., p. 55.
55 See p. 81ff. for discussion of the problems to which this gives rise.
56 Cf. Charlesworth, op. cit., p. 23. For detailed discussion of Anselm's precise relationship to mainstream neo-platonism, see Richard Campbell, 'Anselm's Background Metaphysics', op. cit.
57 'On Worshipping the Right God', in *God and the Soul* (RKP, London 1969), pp. 114-5.

Chapter 4

1 'On What There Is', reprinted in *From a Logical Point of View* (Harvard University Press, Cambridge, Mass. 1953), p. 21.
2 ibid., p. 23.
3 *Principia Mathematica* (George Allen & Unwin, London 1937, 2nd. ed.), p. 449.
4 See for instance J. D. Findlay, *Meinong's Theory of Objects and Values* (Oxford University Press, 1963, 2nd. ed.), p. 47.
5 Reprinted in ed. Alvin Plantinga, *The Ontological Argument* (Macmillan, London 1968), pp. 86-110.
6 ibid., p. 89.
7 ibid., p. 94.
8 ibid., pp. 103-4.
9 op. cit., p. 23.
10 See e.g., Jonathan Barnes, *The Ontological Argument* (Macmillan, London 1972), p. 48.
11 'Degrees of Reality in Plato', in ed. Renford Bambrough, *New Essays on Plato and Aristotle* (RKP, London 1965), p. 7, fn. 5.
12 ibid., pp. 8-9.
13 *Plato's Thought* (Methuen, London 1935), p. 49. Cf. *Plato's 'Phaedo'*, trans. with introduction and commentary by R. Hackforth (Cambridge University Press, 1955), p. 143.
14 op. cit., p. 7.
15 *Republic* 507b.
16 See *Republic* 505b and 508e.
17 *The Problems of Philosophy* (Oxford University Press, 1967), p. 56.
18 *The Spirit of Medieval Philosophy* (Sheed and Ward, London 1936), p. 59.
19 *Systematic Theology* (Nisbet, Welwyn 1968), Vol. I, pp. 261-3.
20 *God and Philosophy* (Yale University Press, New Haven 1959), p. 54.
21 Etienne Gilson, *Reason and Revelation in the Middle Ages* (Charles Scribner's Sons, N.Y. 1939), p. 100. (I am sure Gilson would say the same of supra- or non-spatial existence.)
22 op. cit., pp. 18-19.
23 This disposes of arguments such as that of Robert Oakes in 'The Second Ontological Argument and Existence-*Simpliciter*', *International*

Journal for Philosophy of Religion, 6 (1975), pp. 180-184, that 'having *necessary-existence* as a property does *not* constitute a logically sufficient condition for having *existence* as a property' (p. 184): there is no 'existence-*simpliciter*'.
24 *On Being and Essence*, in *Selected Writings of St. Thomas Aquinas*, trans. with introduction and notes by Robert P. Goodwin (Bobbs-Merrill, Indianapolis 1965), pp. 33-4, a discussion of *Metaphysics*, V, 7, 1017a 22-35.
25 ibid., p. 34. Aquinas continues: 'In another way it signifies the truth of propositions...[and] ...can be attributed to anything concerning which an affirmative proposition can be formed, even if it posits nothing in reality.' But this is not a very helpful way, being an apparent forerunner of the thesis that everything is, but not everything exists.
26 ibid., p. 58 (my italics).
27 *Being and Some Philosophers* (Pontifical Institute of Medieval Studies, Toronto 1952), p. 180.

Chapter 5

1 Cf. Anselm's claim that Christ '*could* not avoid death', which he says refers 'to the *unchangeableness* of his purpose...' (ibid., p. 275, my italics).
2 See ch. 2, p. 28.
3 Hick's arguments are set out in 'A Critique of the "Second Argument"', in ed. Hick and McGill, *The Many-Faced Argument* (Macmillan, London 1968), pp. 341-356 (hereafter CSA); 'God As Necessary Being', *Journal of Philosophy*, 57 (1960), pp. 725-734 (hereafter GNB); and 'Necessary Being', *Scottish Journal of Theology*, 14 (1961), pp. 353-369 (hereafter NB). Hartshorne's position is set out in e.g., 'The Rationale of the Ontological Proof', *Theology Today*, 20 (1963), pp. 278-283 and 'John Hick on Logical and Ontological Necessity', *Religious Studies*, 13 (1977), pp. 155-165. In addition to the writers I discuss, see in support of Hick e.g., R. Campbell, R. L. Franklin, P. Geach, A. Kenny, J. O. Nelson, R. L. Purtill, A. C. A. Rainer, and F. Zabeeh; and for a variety of objections and caveats, W. E. Abraham, R. M. Adams, J. A. Brunton, A. Daher, J. Gaspard, P. A. Hutchings, A. Prior, and J. F. Ross, all as cited in the bibliography.
4 CSA, p. 342.
5 'Has It Been Proved that All Real Existence is Contingent?', *American Philosophical Quarterly*, 8 (1971), p. 287. For more detailed consideration of this analogy see my 'Pure Objects and the Ontological Argument', *Sophia*, 14 (1975), pp. 10-18.
6 CSA, p. 344; cf. GNB, p. 728.
7 'Can God's Existence Be Disproved?', reprinted in ed. A. Plantinga, *The Ontological Argument* (Macmillan, London 1968), p. 117.
8 Raziel Abelson, 'Not Necessarily', *Philosophical Review*, 70 (1961), p. 74.
9 See John Hick, NB, p. 365; cf. GNB, p. 733.
10 According to Hartshorne, his existence, but not his actuality, must

be necessary: see e.g., 'What Did Anselm Discover?', in ed. Hick and McGill, op. cit., pp. 329-333. 'Actuality', or 'concrete existence', is a term he takes from process philosophy, and applies to God in order to differentiate between his (necessary) existence and (contingent) activity, which is part of his notion of 'neo-classical theism'.
11 'What Did Anselm Discover?', op. cit., p. 326.
12 'Anselm's Ontological Arguments', ibid., pp. 307-8. Cf. Aristotle, *De Generatione*, II, 12, 338^a, 1-4: 'For what is "of necessity" coincides with what is "always" since that which "must be" cannot possibly "not-be". Hence a thing is eternal if its "being" is necessary: and if it is eternal, its being is necessary.'
13 ibid., p. 309.
14 Cf. Jérôme Gaspard, 'On the Existence of a Necessary Being', *Journal of Philosophy*, 31 (1934), pp. 5-14, and Alan G. Nasser, 'Factual and Logical Necessity and the Ontological Argument', *International Philosophical Quarterly*, 11 (1971), pp. 385-402.
15 Terence Penelhum, 'On the Second Ontological Argument', *Philosophical Review*, 70 (1961), p. 90.
16 ibid.
17 D. P. Henry, *Medieval Logic and Metaphysics* (Hutchinson, London 1972), pp. 108-9.
18 'A Valid Ontological Argument?', reprinted in ed. A. Plantinga, op. cit., p. 165.
19 ibid., p. 166.
20 ibid., p. 169.
21 ibid., p. 168.
22 ibid., pp. 168-9.
23 ibid., p. 169.
24 ibid.
25 I take Becker's Postulate as accepted: see e.g. Alan Nasser, op. cit., pp. 395-6.
26 CSA, p. 346.
27 ibid.
28 ibid., p. 347; cf. NB, p. 366 and GNB, p. 733.
29 GNB, p. 731.
30 ibid.
31 ibid.
32 CSA, p. 354.
33 ibid., p. 355.
34 ibid., p. 356.
35 For discusssion of this point in connection with Hartshorne's argument see my 'Hartshorne's Modal Argument for the Existence of God', *Ratio*, 27 (1975), pp. 143-4.
36 CSA, pp. 353-4.
37 ibid., p. 356.
38 ibid.
39 GNB, p. 733; cf. NB, p. 366.
40 ibid., p. 732; cf. NB, ibid.
41 ibid.
42 CSA, p. 348; cf. R. Campbell, *From Belief to Understanding*

(Australian National University, Canberra 1978), pp. 116-7.
43   Cf. Charles Hartshorne, 'John Hick on Logical and Ontological Necessity', op. cit., pp. 160-1.
44   op. cit., p. 73.
45   John Hick, GNB, p. 732.
46   See e.g. such philosophers of science as Thomas Kuhn.
47   'A Valid Ontological Argument?', op. cit., pp. 170-1.
48   ibid., p. 171.
49   Malcolm, op. cit., p. 317.
50   Cf. e.g. Jerome Shaffer, 'Existence, Predication, and the Ontological Argument', in Hick and McGill, op. cit., p. 242, where he argues that 'if someone uses the sentence, "God exists" tautologically, he tells us only that being an existent is a logical requirement for being God. If, on the other hand, someone asserts, "God exists" nontautologically, then he claims that the term "God" has extension, applies to some existent. In the case of the Ontological Argument the only valid conclusion is an intensional statement about the meaning of the concept of God.' The point is, however, that in this case, whether or not the term in question, 'God', has an extension, depends on the coherence or otherwise of the intensional statement about 'God'. If God exists, then it is necessarily true that he exists; and whether or not he exists depends upon the possibility of his existing. The logically prior determinant of *this* possibility is the logical coherence or otherwise of its being a logical requirement for x to be God, that x should be an existent.
51   'What Did Anselm Discover?', op. cit., p. 322.
52   op. cit., p. 320.
53   *Physics*, III, 4, 203^b, 30.
54   Bonaventure, *De Myst. Trin.*, I, 1, 29, t.v., p. 48; cited by Etienne Gilson, *The Philosophy of Bonaventure*, trans. by Dom Illtyd Trethowan and F. J. Sheed (Sheed and Ward, London 1940), p. 128.
55   That 'God' is used in (at least) two fundamentally distinct ways both in the scriptures and in theology is not, I take it, controversial; since as e.g. Robin Attfield points out, '...we can make no sense of language about God unless "God" is at least sometimes taken as the name of an individual of a certain sort. But "God" is also sometimes to be taken as the name of the kind of thing God is.' — 'The Individuality of God', *Sophia*, 10 (1971), p. 26. Cf. Michael Durrant, *The Logical Status of 'God'* (Macmillan, London 1973).
56   'On Worshipping the Right God', in Peter Geach, *God and the Soul* (RKP, London 1969), p. 115.

Chapter 6

1   Ludwig Feuerbach, *The Essence of Christianity* (Harper and Row, N.Y. 1957), p. 213. Cf. pp. 13-25.
2   Kai Nielsen, *Contemporary Critiques of Religion* (Macmillan, London 1971), p. 14.

Bibliography

Anselmian texts

Opera Omnia, ed. by Dom F. S. Schmitt (Nelson & Sons, Edinburgh, 6 vols., 1945–51)
Anselm of Canterbury, vol. I, ed. and trans. by Jasper Hopkins and Herbert Richardson (SCM, London 1974)
St. Anselm: Basic Writings, trans. by S. N. Deane (Open Court, La Salle, Ill. 1962, 2nd ed.)
St. Anselm's 'Proslogion' with 'A Reply on Behalf of the Fool' and 'The Author's Reply to Gaunilo', trans., with an introduction and philosophical commentary, by M. J. Charlesworth (Oxford University Press, 1965)
Dialogue on Truth, in *Selections from Medieval Philosophers*, ed. and trans., with introductory notes, by Richard McKeon (Charles Scribner's Sons, N.Y. 1929)

Books

An Aquinas Reader, ed., with an introduction, by Mary T. Clark (Hodder & Stoughton, London 1972)
Selected Writings of St. Thomas Aquinas, trans., with an introduction and notes, by Robert P. Goodwin (Bobbs-Merrill, Indianapolis 1965)
Austin, J. L. *Sense and Sensibilia*, ch. VII (Oxford University Press, 1962)
Barnes, Jonathan. *The Ontological Argument* (Macmillan, London 1972)
Barth, Karl. *Anselm: Fides Quaerens Intellectum*, trans. by Ian Robertson (SCM, London 1960)
Barth, Karl. *Church Dogmatics*, I, 1; I, 2; II, 1 (T. & T. Clark, Edinburgh 1936 onwards)
Campbell, Richard. *From Belief to Understanding* (Australian National University, Canberra 1976)
Collingwood, R. G. *Philosophical Method* (Oxford University Press, 1933)
Durrant, Michael. *The Logical Status of 'God'* (Macmillan, London 1973)

Durrant, Michael. *Theology and Intelligibility* (RKP, London 1973)
Evans, G. R. *Anselm and Talking about God* (Oxford University Press, 1978)
Geach, Peter. *God and the Soul* (RKP, London 1969)
Gilson, Etienne. *Being and Some Philosophers* (Pontifical Institute of Medieval Studies, Toronto 1952, 2nd. ed.)
Gilson, Etienne. *God and Philosophy* (Yale University Press, New Haven 1944)
Gombocz, W. *Über E! Zur Semantik des Existenzprädikates und des Ontologischen Argumentes für Gottes Existenz von Anselm von Canterbury* (Universität Graz, Vienna 1974)
Hartshorne, Charles. *Anselm's Discovery* (Open Court, La Salle, Ill. 1965)
Hartshorne, Charles. *The Logic of Perfection and Other Essays in Neoclassical Metaphysics* (Open Court, La Salle, Ill. 1962)
Hartshorne, Charles. *A Natural Theology for Our Time* (Open Court, La Salle, Ill. 1967)
Henry, D. P. *The Logic of St. Anselm* (Oxford University Press, 1967)
Henry, D. P. *Medieval Logic and Metaphysics* (Hutchinson, London 1972)
Hick, John, ed. *Faith and the Philosophers* (Macmillan, London 1966)
Hick, John and McGill, Arthur C., eds. *The Many-Faced Argument* (Macmillan, London 1968)
Hopkins, Jasper. *A Companion to the Study of St. Anselm* (University of Minnesota, Minneapolis 1972)
Koyré, Alexandre. *L'Idée de Dieu dans la Philosophie de S. Anselme* (J. Vrin, Paris 1923)
La Croix, Richard R. *Proslogion II and III* (E. J. Brill, Leiden 1972)
Lovejoy, Arthur O. *The Great Chain of Being* (Harper and Row, N.Y. 1960)
McIntyre, John. *St. Anselm and His Critics* (Oliver & Boyd, Edinburgh 1954)
Phelan, P. *The Wisdom of St. Anselm* (Archabbey Press, Latrobe, Pa. 1960)
Phillips, D. Z. *Faith and Philosophical Inquiry* (RKP, London 1970)
Plantinga, Alvin. *God, Freedom, and Evil* (Harper and Row, N.Y. 1974)
Plantinga, Alvin. *God and Other Minds* (Cornell University Press, Ithaca 1967)
Plantinga, Alvin. *The Nature of Necessity* (Oxford University Press, 1974)
Plantinga, Alvin, ed. *The Ontological Argument* (Macmillan, London 1968)
Plato. *Republic*, vol. 4 of *The Dialogues of Plato*, trans. by Benjamin Jowett (Sphere Books, London 1970)
Schmitt, Dom F. S., ed. *Analecta Anselmiana* (Minerva, Frankfurt 1968)
Southern, R. W., ed. *Eadmer, The Life of St. Anselm* (Nelson, London 1962)
Southern, R. W. *St. Anselm and His Biographer* (Cambridge University Press, 1963)
Southern, R. W. and Schmitt, F. S., ed. *Memorials of St. Anselm* (Oxford University Press, 1969)

Webb, C. C. J. *Studies in the History of Natural Theology* (Oxford University Press, 1970)

Articles

Abraham, W. E. 'Is the Concept of Necessary Existence Self-Contradictory?', *Inquiry*, 5 (1962), pp. 143–157

Adams, R. M. 'Has it been Proved that all Real Existence is Contingent?', *American Philosophical Quarterly*, 8 (1971), pp. 284–291

Adams, R. M. 'Theories of Actuality', *Nous*, 8 (1974), pp. 211–231

Alston, William P. 'The Ontological Argument Revisited', *Philosophical Review*, 69 (1960), pp. 452–474. Reprinted in ed. A. Plantinga, *The Ontological Argument* (Macmillan, London 1968), pp. 86–110

Angluin, D. J. C. 'Austin's Mistake about "Real"', *Philosophy*, 49 (1974), pp. 47–62

Attfield, Robin. 'The Individuality of God', *Sophia*, 10 (1971), pp. 20–27

Attfield, Robin. 'The Lord is God: There is No Other', *Religious Studies*, 13 (1977), pp. 73–84

Balthasar, N. 'Idéalisme anselmien et réalisme thomiste', *Annales de l'Institut Supérieur de Philosophie* (Louvain), 1 (1912), pp. 431–467

Barnette, R. L. 'Anselm and the Fool', *International Philosophical Quarterly*, 6 (1975), pp. 201–218

Baumer, W. H. 'Anselm, Truth and Necessary Being', *Philosophy*, 37 (1962), pp. 257–258

Beckaert, A. 'Une justification platonicienne de l'argument a priori', *Spicilegium Beccense* (J. Vrin, Paris 1959), pp. 185–190. Trans. in ed. J. Hick and A. C. McGill, *The Many-Faced Argument* (Macmillan, London 1968), pp. 111–118

Bergenthal, Ferdinand. 'Ist Der "Ontologische Gottesbeweis" Anselms von Canterbury ein Trugschluss?', *Philosophisches Jahrbuch*, 59 (1949), pp. 155–168

Bishop, D. H. 'Anselm and his Critics – a Critique', *Journal of Thought*, 9 (1974), pp. 155–157

Bouillard, Henri. 'La Preuve de Dieu dans le "Proslogion" et son interprétation par Karl Barth', *Spicilegium Beccense* (J. Vrin, Paris 1959), pp. 191–207

Bouwsma, O. K. 'Anselm's Argument', in ed. Joseph Bobik, *The Nature of Philosophical Inquiry* (Notre Dame University Press, Indiana 1970), pp. 252–293

Brecher, R. 'Aquinas on Anselm', *Philosophical Studies* (Eire), XXIII (1975), pp. 63–66

Brecher, R. '"Greatness" in Anselm's Ontological Argument', *Philosophical Quarterly*, 24 (1974), pp. 97–105

Brecher, R. 'Gremlins and Parodies', *Philosophical Studies* (Eire), XXX (1982), pp. 48–54

Brecher, R. 'Hartshorne's Modal Argument for the Existence of God', *Ratio*, 17 (1976), pp. 140–146

Brecher, R. 'Pure Objects and the Ontological Argument', *Sophia*, 14 (1975), pp. 10–18

Brown, T. P. 'Prof. Malcolm on "Anselm's Ontological Arguments"', *Analysis*, 22 (1961), pp. 12—14

Brunton, J. A. 'The Logic of God's Necessary Existence', *International Philosophical Quarterly*, 10, (1970), pp. 276—290

Caird, Edward. 'Anselm's Argument for the Being of God', *The Journal of Theological Studies*, 1 (1899), pp. 23—39

Campbell, Richard. 'Anselm's Background Metaphysics', *Scottish Journal of Theology*, 33 (1980), pp. 317—343

Campbell, Richard. 'Anselm's Theological Method', *Scottish Journal of Theology*, 32 (1979), pp. 541—562

Campbell, Richard. 'Real Predicates and "Exists"', *Mind*, 83 (1974), pp. 95—99

Cappuyns, D. M. 'L'Argument de S. Anselme', *Récherches de théologie ancienne et médievale*, 6 (1934), pp. 313—330

Cargile, James. 'The Ontological Argument', *Philosophy*, 50 (1975), pp. 69—80

Carter, W. R. 'Plantinga on Existing Necessarily', *Canadian Journal of Philosophy*, 6 (1976), pp. 95—104

Chopra, Y. N. 'Worshipping the Right God', *Philosophy*, 50 (1975), pp. 94—96

Coburn, R. C. 'Prof. Malcolm on God', *Australasian Journal of Philosophy*, 41 (1963), pp. 153—162

Cock, Albert A. 'The Ontological Argument for the Existence of God', *PAS*, 18 (1918), pp. 363—384

Cosgrove, Matthew R. 'Thomas Aquinas on Anselm's Argument', *Review of Metaphysics*, 27 (1974), pp. 513—530

Crocker, Sylvia Fleming. 'The Ontological Significance of Anselm's "Proslogion"', *The Modern Schoolman*, 50 (1972), pp. 33—56

Daher, Adel. 'God and Factual Necessity', *Religious Studies*, 6 (1970), pp. 23—39

Davies, A. E. 'The Problem of Truth and Existence as Treated by Anselm', *PAS*, 20 (1920), pp. 167—190

Davis, S. T. 'Anselm and Gaunilo on the "Lost Island"', *Southern Journal of Philosophy*, 13 (1975), pp. 435—448

Devine, Philip E. 'Does St. Anselm Beg the Question?', *Philosophy*, 50 (1975), pp. 271—281

Devine, Philip E. 'The Perfect Island, The Devil, and Existent Unicorns', *American Philosophical Quarterly*, 12 (1975), pp. 255—260

Devine, Philip E. 'The Real Significance of the Ontological Argument', *Religious Studies*, 11 (1975), pp. 97—116

Doyle, J. P. 'St. Bonaventure and the Ontological Argument', *The Modern Schoolman*, 52 (1974), pp. 27—48

Duncan, Roger. 'Analogy and the Ontological Argument', *New Scholasticism*, 54 (1980), pp. 25—33

Findlay, J. N. 'Can God's Existence be Disproved?', *Mind*, 57 (1948), pp. 176—183. Reprinted in ed. Antony Flew and Alasdair McIntyre, *New Essays in Philosophical Theology* (SCM, London 1958), pp. 47—56, and in ed. A. Plantinga, *The Ontological Argument* (Macmillan, London 1968), pp. 111—122

Replies and Rejoinder:

Hughes, G. E. 'Has God's Existence been Disproved?', in ed. A. Flew and A. McIntyre, op. cit., pp. 56–67

Rainer, A. C. A. 'Necessity and God', ibid., pp. 67–71

Findlay, J. N. 'God's Non-Existence: A Reply to Mr. Rainer and Mr. Hughes', ibid., pp. 71–5

Fischer, J. 'Die Erkenntnislehre Anselms von Canterbury', in *Beiträge zur Geschichte der Philosophie des Mittelalters*, 10, 3 (Aschendorffsche Verlagsbuchhandlung, Münster 1911

Franklin, R. L. 'Necessary Being', *Australasian Journal of Philosophy*, 35 (1957), pp. 97–100

Gaspard, Jerome. 'On the Existence of a Necessary Being', *Journal of Philosophy*, 31 (1934), pp. 5–14

Gilson, Etienne. 'Sens et nature de l'argument de Saint Anselme', *Archives d'histoire doctrinale et litteraire du moyen age*, 9 (1934), pp. 5–51

Grant, C. K. 'The Ontological Disproof of the Devil', *Analysis*, 17 (1957), pp. 71–2

Discussion:

Richman, Robert J. 'The Ontological Proof of the Devil', *Philosophical Studies*, 9 (1958), pp. 63–64

Waldman, Theodore. 'A Comment Upon the Ontological Proof of the Devil', ibid., 10 (1959), pp. 59–60

Richman, Robert J. 'The Devil and Dr. Waldman', ibid., 11 (1960), pp. 78–80

Johnson, Oliver A. 'God and St. Anselm', *Journal of Religion*, 45 (1965), pp. 326–334

Haight, David and Marjorie. 'An Ontological Argument for the Devil', *The Monist*, 54 (1970), pp. 218–220

Gombocz, Wolfgang. 'St. Anselm's Disproof of the Devil's Existence. A Counter Argument Against Haight and Richman', *Ratio*, 15 (1973), pp. 334–337

Richman, Robert J. 'A Serious Look at the Ontological Argument', ibid., 18 (1976), pp. 85–89

Gombocz, Wolfgang, 'St. Anselm's Two Devils But One God', ibid., 20 (1978), pp. 142–146

Wainwright, W. J. 'On an Alleged Incoherence in Anselm's Argument: A Reply to Robert Richman', ibid., pp. 147–148

Rabinowicz, Wlodzimierz. 'An Alleged New Refutation of St. Anselm's Argument', ibid., pp. 149–150

Grim, Patrick. 'Plantinga's God and Other Monstrosities', *Religious Studies*, 15 (1979), pp. 91–97

Hardin, C. L. 'An Empirical Refutation of the Ontological Argument', *Analysis*, 22 (1961), pp. 10–12

Reply:

Resnick, L. 'A Logical Refutation of Mr. Hardin's Argument', ibid., 23 (1962), pp. 90–91

Hartford, R. R. 'Fides Quaerens Intellectum', *Hermathena*, 74 (1949), pp. 1–8

Hartshorne, Charles. 'The Formal Validity and Real Significance of the Ontological Argument', *Philosophical Review*, 53 (1944), pp. 225–245

Replies and Rejoinders:
Elton, William. 'On Hartshorne's Formulation of the Ontological Argument', *Philosophical Review*, 54 (1945), pp. 63—65
Elton, William. 'Professor Hartshorne's Syllogism', ibid., pp. 506—508
Hartshorne, Charles. 'The Idea of God...Literal or Analogical?', *The Christian Scholar* (1956), pp. 131—136
Hartshorne, Charles. 'John Hick on Logical and Ontological Necessity', *Religious Studies*, 13 (1977), pp. 73—84
Hartshorne, Charles. 'The Logic of the Ontological Argument', *Journal of Philosophy*, 58 (1961), pp. 471—473
Hartshorne, Charles. 'The Rationale of the Ontological Proof', *Theology Today*, 20 (1963), pp. 278—283
Hartshorne, Charles. 'What Did Anselm Discover?', in ed. J. Hick and A. C. McGill, *The Many-Faced Argument* (Macmillan, London 1968), pp. 321—333
Hayen, André. 'Anselme et Thomas. La Vraie nature de la théologie et sa portée apostolique', *Spicilegium Beccense*, (J. Vrin, Paris 1959). Trans. in ed. J. Hick and A. C. McGill, *The Many-Faced Argument* (Macmillan, London 1968), pp. 162—182
Henry, D. P. 'Proslogion Chapter III', in ed. F. S. Schmitt, *Analecta Anselmiana* (Minerva, Frankfurt 1968), pp. 101—105
Henry, D. P. 'The "Proslogion" Proofs', *Philosophical Quarterly*, 5 (1955), pp. 147—151
Henry, D. P. 'St. Anselm's Nonsense', *Mind*, 72 (1963), pp. 51—60
Henry, D. P. 'Was St. Anselm Really a Realist?', *Ratio*, 5 (1963), pp. 181—189
Hick, John. 'A Critique of the "Second Argument"' in ed. J. Hick and A. C. McGill, *The Many-Faced Argument* (Macmillan, London 1968), pp. 341—356
Hick, John. 'God as Necessary Being', *Journal of Philosophy*, 57 (1960), pp. 725—734
Hick, John. 'Necessary Being', *Scottish Journal of Theology*, 14 (1961), pp. 353—369
Hochberg, Herbert. 'St. Anselm's Ontological Argument and Russell's Theory of Descriptions', *The New Scholasticism*, 33 (1959), pp. 319—330
Hopkins, Jasper. 'On Understanding and Preunderstanding St. Anselm', *The New Scholasticism*, 52 (1978), pp. 243—260
Horgan, John. 'L'abstraction de l'être', *Révue néo-scholastique de philosophie* (1939), pp. 161—181
Huggett, W. J. 'The "Proslogion" Proof Re-examined', *Indian Journal of Philosophy*, 2 (1960—1), pp. 193—202
Humber, James. 'Causal Necessity and the Ontological Argument', *Religious Studies*, 10 (1974), pp. 291—300
Hutchings, P. A. 'Necessary Being', *Australasian Journal of Philosophy* 35 (1957), pp. 201—206
Hutchings, P. A. 'Necessary Being and Some Types of Tautology', *Philosophy*, 39 (1964), pp. 1—17
Johnson, J. Prescott. 'The Ontological Argument in Plato', *The Personalist*, 44 (1963), pp. 24—34

Kenny, Anthony. 'Necessary Being', *Sophia*, 1 (1962), pp. 1–8
Kenny, Anthony. 'God and Necessity', in ed. Bernard Williams and Alan Montefiore, *British Analytical Philosophy* (RKP, London 1966), pp. 131–151
King-Farlow, J. 'Existence and Proving Gods', *Darshana*, 1 (1961), pp. 46–58
Kiteley, M. 'Existence and the Ontological Argument', *Philosophy and Phenomenological Research*, 18 (1958), pp. 533–534
Kuhlmann, Gerhardt. 'Zu Karl Barths Anselmbuch', *Zeitschrift für Theologie and Kirche*, 13 (1932), pp. 269–281
Lewis, David. 'Anselm and Actuality', *Nous*, 4 (1970), pp. 175–188
McIntyre, John. 'The System of St. Anselm's Theology', *Spicilegium Beccense* (J. Vrin, Paris 1959)
Malcolm, Norman. 'Anselm's Ontological Arguments', *Philosophical Review*, 69 (1960), pp. 41–62. Reprinted in ed. J. Hick and A. C. McGill, *The Many-Faced Argument* (Macmillan, London 1968), pp. 301–320, and in ed. A. Plantinga, *The Ontological Argument* (Macmillan, London 1968), pp. 136–139
Discussion:
Allen, R. E. 'Ontological Argument', *Philosophical Review*, 70 (1961), pp. 56–66
Abelson, Raziel. 'Not Necessarily', ibid., pp. 67–84
Henle, Paul. 'Uses of the Ontological Argument', ibid., pp. 102–109
Matthews, Gareth. 'On Conceivability in Anselm and Malcolm', ibid., pp. 110–111
Penelhum, Terence. 'On the Second Ontological Argument', ibid., pp. 85–89
Plantinga, Alvin. 'A Valid Ontological Argument?', ibid., pp. 93–101
Mann, William. 'The Ontological Presuppositions of the Ontological Argument', *Review of Metaphysics*, 25 (1972), pp. 260–277
Mascall, E. L. 'Faith and Reason: Anselm and Aquinas', *Journal of Theological Studies*, 14 (1963), pp. 67–90
Matthews, Gareth. 'Aquinas on Saying God Doesn't Exist', *The Monist*, 47 (1963), pp. 472–477
Miethe, T. L. 'The Ontological Argument: A Research Bibliography', *The Modern Schoolman*, 54 (1977), pp. 148–166
Miller, Paul J. W. 'The Ontological Argument for God', *The Personalist*, 42 (1961), pp. 337–351
Miller, Robert G. 'The Ontological Argument in St. Anselm and Descartes', *The Modern Schoolman*, 32 (1955), pp. 341–349, and 33 (1956), pp. 31–38
Nasser, A. G. 'Factual and Logical Necessity and the Ontological Argument', *International Philosophical Quarterly*, 11 (1971), pp. 385–402
Nelson, J. O. 'Modal Logic and the Ontological Proof of God's Existence', *Review of Metaphysics*, 16 (1963), pp. 235–242
Reply: Hartshorne, Charles. 'What the Ontological Proof Does Not Do', *Review of Metaphysics*, 17 (1964), pp. 608–609
Oakes, Robert. 'The Second Ontological Argument and Existence-Simpliciter', *International Journal for Philosophy of Religion*, 6 (1975), pp. 180–184

O'Gorman, F. P. 'Yet Another Look at the Ontological Argument', *Philosophical Studies* (Eire), vol. XXIII (1975), pp. 49–62

Pailin, David A. 'An Introductory Survey of Charles Hartshorne's Work on the Ontological Argument', in ed. F. S. Schmitt, *Analecta Anselmiana* (Minerva, Frankfurt 1968), pp. 195–221

Penelhum, Terence. 'Divine Necessity', *Mind*, 69 (1960), pp. 175–186

Plantinga, Alvin. 'Kant's Objection to the Ontological Argument', *Journal of Philosophy*, 63 (1966), pp. 536–546

Prior, Arthur. 'Is Necessary Existence Possible?', *Philosophy and Phenomenological Research*, 15 (1955), pp. 545–547

Pucetti, Roland. 'The Concept of God', *Philosophical Quarterly*, 14 (1964), pp. 237–245

Purtill, R. L. 'Hartshorne's Modal Proof', *Journal of Philosophy*, 63 (1966), pp. 397–409
  Reply with rejoinder and second reply: Hartshorne, Charles. 'Necessity', *Review of Metaphysics*, 21 (1967), pp. 290–309

Purtill, R. L. 'Plantinga, Necessity and God', *New Scholasticism*, 50 (1976), pp. 46–60
  Reply: Plantinga, Alvin. 'Existence, Necessity, and God', ibid., pp. 61–72

Purtill, R. L. 'Three Ontological Arguments', *International Journal for Philosophy of Religion*, 6 (1975), pp. 102–110

Quine, W. V. O. 'On What There Is', reprinted in W. V. O. Quine, *From A Logical Point of View* (Harvard University Press, Cambridge, Mass. 1953)

Richardson, Cyril C. 'The Strange Fascination of the Ontological Argument', *Union Seminary Quarterly Review*, 18 (1962), pp. 1–21
  Discussion:
  Brkic, Joran. ibid., pp. 246–249
  Comstock, Richard W. ibid., pp. 250–255
  Hartshorne, Charles. ibid., pp. 244–245

Ross, J. F. 'God and "Logical Necessity"', *Philosophical Quarterly*, 11 (1961), pp. 22–27

Ross, J. F. 'Logically Necessary Existential Statements', *Journal of Philosophy*, 58 (1961), pp. 253–262

Rowe, W. L. 'The Ontological Argument and Question-Begging', *International Journal for Philosophy of Religion*, 7 (1976), pp. 425–432
  Replies and Rejoinder:
  Davis, S. T. 'Does the Ontological Argument Beg the Question?', ibid., pp. 433–442
  Rowe, W. L. 'Comments on Professor Davis' "Does the Ontological Argument Beg the Question?"', ibid., pp. 443–447
  Davis, S. T. 'Anselm and Question-Begging: A Reply to William Rowe', ibid., pp. 448–457

Samuel, Otto. 'Der Ontologische Gottesbeweis bei Karl Barth, Immanuel Kant, und Anselm von Canterbury', *Theologische Blätter*, 14 (1935), pp. 141–153

Samuelson, Norbert. 'On Proving God's Existence', *Judaism*, 16 (1967), pp. 21–36

Schmitt, F. S. 'Der Ontologische Gottesbeweis Anselms', *Theologische*

Revue, 32 (1933), pp. 217–223
Schufreider, G. 'The Identity of Anselm's Argument', *The Modern Schoolman*, 54 (1977), pp. 345–361
Shaffer, Jerome. 'Existence, Predication, and the Ontological Argument', *Mind*, 71 (1962), pp. 307–325. Reprinted in ed. J. Hick and A. C. McGill, *The Many-Faced Argument* (Macmillan, London 1968), pp. 226–245
Sheldon, W. H. 'Necessary Truths and the Necessary Being', *Journal of Philosophy*, 26 (1929), pp. 197–209
Smart, Hugh R. 'Anselm's Ontological Argument: Rationalistic or Apologetic?', *Review of Metaphysics*, 3 (1949), pp. 161–166
Stolz, A. 'Das Proslogion des hl. Anselm', *Révue Bénédictine*, 47 (1935), pp. 331–347
Stolz, A. '"Vere esse" im Proslogion des hl. Anselm', *Scholastik*, 9 (1934), pp. 400–409
Stolz, A. 'Zur Theologie Anselms im Proslogion', *Catholica*, 1 (1933), pp. 1–24. Trans. in ed. J. Hick and A. C. McGill, *The Many-Faced Argument* (Macmillan, London 1968), pp. 183–206
Tillich, Paul. 'The Two Types of Philosophy of Religion', in Paul Tillich, *Theology of Culture* (Oxford University Press, N.Y. 1959), pp. 10–29
Toohey, John J. 'The Term "Being"', *The New Scholasticism*, 16 (1942), pp. 107–129
Vergnes, Jules. 'Les sources de l'argument de saint Anselme', *Révue des Sciences Réligieuses*, 4 (1924), pp. 576–579
Vlastos, Gregory. 'Degrees of Reality in Plato', in ed. Renford Bambrough, *New Essays on Plato and Aristotle* (RKP, London 1965), pp. 1–20
Vuillemin, Jules. 'Id quo nihil maius cogitari potest. Über die innere Möglichkeit eines rationales Gottesbegriffs', *Archiv für Geschichte der Philosophie*, 53 (1971), pp. 279–299
Webb, C. C. J. 'Anselm's Ontological Argument for the Existence of God', *PAS*, 3 (1896), pp. 25–43
Werner, Charles G. 'The Ontological Argument for the Existence of God', *The Personalist*, 46 (1965), pp. 269–283
Wolz, Henry G. 'The Function of Faith in the Ontological Argument', *Proceedings of the American Catholic Philosophical Association*, 25 (1951), pp. 151–163
Yolton, John W. 'Prof. Malcolm on St. Anselm, Belief, and Existence', *Philosophy*, 36 (1961), pp. 367–370
Young, J. Michael. 'The Ontological Argument and the Concept of Substance', *American Philosophical Quarterly*, 11 (1974), pp. 181–191
Zabeeh, Farhang. 'On Necessary Existence', *Indian Journal of Philosophy*, 3 (1962), pp. 227–233
Zabeeh, Farhang. 'Ontological Argument and How and Why Some Speak of God', *Philosophy and Phenomenological Research*, 22 (1961), pp. 206–215
Reply and Rejoinder:
Hartshorne, Charles. 'How Some Speak and Yet Do Not Speak of God', *ibid.*, 23 (1962), pp. 274–276
Zabeeh, Farhang. 'Category-Mistake', *ibid.*, pp. 277–279
Ziff, Paul. 'About God', in ed. Sidney Hook, *Religious Experience and Truth* (Oliver & Boyd, Edinburgh 1962)

Index of names

Abelson, R.   100-1
Adams, R.M.   88
Alexander of Hales   3
Alston, W.   72-5
Anselm   3, 4, 5, 6-17, 19-35,
  36-69, 78, 79, 80, 81, 82,
  83, 85-8, 90, 91, 92, 97,
  103, 105-13, 115, 116, 120n
Aquinas   3, 52, 53-7, 83,
  123n, 125n
Aristotle   21, 78, 83, 105,
  126n
Attfield, R.   127n
Augustine   10, 11, 118n

Barnes, J.   16, 124n
Barth, K.   3, 4, 38, 42, 44-8,
  117n, 122n
Boethius   25
Bonaventure   3, 16, 108,
  118n

Caird, E.   3
Campbell, R.   4, 38-40, 42,
  43, 118n, 120n, 121n, 124n
Caterus   16
Charlesworth, M.   8, 58-9,
  117n, 120n
Cock, A.A.   119n
Cosgrove, M.   53-5, 122n
Crocker, S.F.   117n

Daniels, A.   117n, 118n
Descartes, R.   3, 9, 56, 117n

Durrant, M.   127n

Feuerbach, L.   114
Findlay, J.N.   89, 95, 96, 124n
Fishacre, R.   3

Gassendi, P.   3, 16
Gaunilo   3, 5, 8, 15-17, 39,
  43, 47, 48, 52-4, 57, 64,
  109, 111, 120n
Geach, P.   67, 113, 127n
Gilson, E.   3, 78, 79, 83,
  118n, 124n
Gombocz, W.L.   119n
Grant, C.K.   17

Haight, D. and M.   119n
Hartshorne, C.   3, 19, 20-30,
  32, 35, 54, 89, 92, 103-5,
  117n, 125n
Hayen, A.   117n
Hegel, G.W.F.   3
Henry, D.P.   21, 61, 119n,
  120n
Hick, J.   88, 89, 95-9, 125n
Hobbes, T.   3
Hopkins, J.   43, 120n, 121n
Hume, D.   86, 88, 92

Johnson, O.A.   119n

Kant, I.   3, 5, 67, 86, 90, 92
Koyré, A.   3
Kuhn, T.   127n

137

La Croix, R.R.   4, 38, 42, 112, 121n
Leibniz, G.W.   3, 67

Malcolm, N.   3, 8, 13, 18, 19, 20, 23, 28, 29, 32, 35, 89, 92-6, 103-5, 120n
Matthews, G.   54-6, 121n
McGill, A.   32
McKeon, R.   122n
Miller, P.J.W.   60, 117n, 118n

Nielsen, K.   127n

Oakes, R.   124n

Penelhum, T.   93
Peter, St   46
Plantinga, A.   63-5, 94-9, 102-3, 118n, 123n
Plato   5, 11, 13, 52, 60, 67-9, 76-8, 80, 82
Plotinus   11

Quine, W.V.O.   71, 73-5, 80

Rabinowicz, W.   119n
Reichenbach, H.   16
Richman, R.J.   17, 119n
Russell, B.   71, 78

Schiller, F.   118n
Schopenhauer, A.   16, 67, 118n
Scotus, D.   3
Seneca   11
Shaffer, J.   127n
Southern, R.W.   117n
Spinoza, B.   3, 114
Stolz, A.   11, 42, 117n, 118n

Tillich, P.   79

Vlastos, G.   13, 76, 77, 78, 80

Wainwright, W.J.   119n
Waldman, T.   119n